THE LITTLE BLACK BOOK OF

WRITERS' WISDOM

THE LITTLE BLACK BOOK OF

WRITERS' WISDOM

Edited by Steven D. Price

Skyhorse Publishing

Skyhorse Publishing books may be purchased in bulk at special discounts for sales promotion, corporate gifts, fund-raising, or educational purposes. Special editions can also be created to specifications. For details, contact the Special Sales Department, Skyhorse Publishing, 307 West 36th Street, 11th Floor, New York, NY 10018 or info@skyhorsepublishing.com.

Skyhorse® and Skyhorse Publishing® are registered trademarks of Skyhorse Publishing, Inc.®, a Delaware corporation.

Visit our website at www.skyhorsepublishing.com.

10 9 8 7 6 5 4 3 2 1

Library of Congress Cataloging-in-Publication Data is available on file.

ISBN: 978-1-5107-7260-1

Printed in China

Contents

Introduction

I started writing professionally some five decades ago. I had been working for a magazine best described as an ill-fated exercise in liberal journalism, my role being to make book deals for the magazine's writers. But then the magazine went belly-up with a combination of a bang and a whimper.

The country was going through a mini-recession, and jobs were scarce, especially in the book publishing industry. I cast about for something— anything—to do, but with no success.

"Why don't you try writing books?" several well-meaning friends suggested.

"But I don't know enough to write a book," I protested.

"But you've been in book publishing long enough to know that you don't have to know everything about a subject. Just pick a subject that you know something about and like a lot."

I had indeed been in book publishing for a while, first as a lawyer, then subsidiary rights salesman, and then editor. And so I gave writing a shot. (Knowing many people in publishing gave me a leg up in getting to editors, who might have considered my book proposal a bit more kindly than if I had been a stranger.) I knew something about horses and liked horse sports a lot, so that was the first subject about which I wrote. Then law, country music, and fishing. I had something to say about those subjects or I collaborated with experts who knew far more than I but needed help in expressing themselves.

My most recent category has been, for the want of a better term, words: I've cobbled together collections of quotations and phrases. All of which have given me a familiarity with the creative and editorial processes and with . . . words.

With all due respect to religious believers, "In the beginning was The Word" has a metaphorical meaning: Civilization began when mankind was first able to communicate by writing. Unlike the earlier oral tradition, an account of any kind—history, fable, law—now could be told when the teller was absent and even after his death.

Chisels, then styli followed by quills, pens, typewriters, and now computers. Clay tablets, then papyrus followed by parchment, paper, and now computers. Technology changes, but contents endure . . . and proliferate.

It's no small wonder that there are more written words than ever before. How many times have you heard someone tell someone in earshot, "What an interesting life [or idea or adventure]—you should write a book." (With a change in pronoun, the speaker could refer to himself or herself.) Although not everyone acts on the suggestion, the avalanche of books published each year through both established publishers and self-publishing, and a similar inundation of blogs and social network postings, indicate that the creative spirit is alive and well. And why shouldn't it be, given the ease with which we can make ourselves heard? "Click and send" isn't exactly heavy lifting.

Ask writers why they write and you'll receive a range of answers. As you'll see in this book's opening chapter, an obsessive need is a recurring and major theme. Take, for example, this line in Hemingway's *Green Hills of Africa*, where the author may indeed be having the character speak for him as well: "I have a good life but I must write because if I do not write a certain amount I do not enjoy the rest of my life."

This book isn't a how-to writing manual; no unseen hand will guide your pen across paper or your fingers on a keyboard. For that you must look elsewhere, to creative writing websites, manuals, and courses. However, writers and critics have never been shy about sharing the tools of their trade, and the "How We Write" chapter offers a wide range of tips, many of which are likely to help your creative and organizational efforts. Similarly, the chapters on fiction and poetry apply to those specialized areas.

Once upon a time, writing letters was as widespread as blogging, texting, and e-mailing are today (epistolary novels were also popular). The practice required thought and expression, with no emoticons and "LOL-type" clichéd abbreviations to take the place of more imaginative writing. Oh well, gone are the days.

What would writers be without editors? Although some would be much happier, I for one am delighted that both sets of creatures exist. I've worked both sides of the street as a writer for and an editor of books and magazines, so that years of participation and observation have borne out the truth of the old line that "bad writers fear them, but good writers prize them." Editors have sharpened my critical faculties and made me a better writer, and I'd like to think I've helped writers and authors along the way. (A note to self-published authors: If you don't have a real live editor helping you, find another pair of eyes and listen to that person's comments. You may not agree with all of them, but your finished product will benefit.)

As for critics, even a bad review means that your work was noticed. You may also learn something about your writing from the reviewer. And if it's a good review with a quotable line that can be used in a "pick-me-up-and-buy-me" blurb, congratulations—you've found heaven on earth.

This book concludes with some light but hardheaded advice, first about writing for money and then a mixed bag of amusing guidance but with a useful edge.

That Hemingway *Green Hills of Africa* line is followed by the character being asked, "And what do you want?"

The answer: "To write as well as I can and learn as I go along. At the same time I have my life which I enjoy and which is a damned good life."

May it be ever thus.

Steven D. Price
New York, N.Y.
July 2012

Acknowledgments

Nick Lyons, who came up with the idea for this book and the recommendation that I do it.

Tony Lyons, Skyhorse's publisher, who agreed.

The many people who over the years advanced my reading and writing skills: Rose Myiofis Price, my mother; William Gordon, my "Uncle Bill"; Dr. Earl Robacker of White Plains High School; Ralph Kaufman of the University of Rochester; Fred Rodell of the Yale Law School.

Gladys S. Topkis, Sandi Gelles-Cole, Alexander MacKay-Smith, Barbara Burn Dolensek, Les Woodcock, William C. Steinkraus, Michael V. Korda, Jacqueline Kennedy Onassis, and Norman M. Fine.

Sara Kitchen, my editor and colleague.

chapter one

"The Inner Music": Why We Write (and Read)

What really knocks me out is a book that, when you're all done reading it, you wish the author that wrote it was a terrific friend of yours and you could call him up on the phone whenever you felt like it. That doesn't happen much, though.
—J. D. SALINGER

• • •

I think I am starving for publication: I love to get published; it maddens me not to get published. I feel at times like getting every publisher in the world by the scruff of the neck, forcing his jaws open, and cramming the Mss down his throat— "God-damn you, here it is—I will and must be published!"

You know what it means—you're a writer and you understand it. It's not just "the satisfaction of being published." Great God! It's the satisfaction of getting it out, or having that, so far as you're concerned, gone through with it! That good or ill, for better or for worse, it's over, done with, finished, out of your life forever and that, come what may, you can at least, as far as this thing is concerned, get the merciful damned easement of oblivion and forgetfulness.
—TOM WOLFE

• • •

Why do writers write? Because it isn't there.
—THOMAS BERGER

• • •

Would you not like to try all sorts of lives—one is so very small—but that is the satisfaction of writing—one can impersonate so many people.
—KATHERINE MANSFIELD

• • •

Writing is an adventure. To begin with, it is a toy and an amusement. Then it becomes a mistress, then it becomes a master, then it becomes a tyrant. The last phase is that just as you are about to be reconciled to your servitude, you kill the monster and fling him to the public.
—WINSTON CHURCHILL

• • •

It wasn't only that this writing seemed beautiful. . . . What made Madeleine sit up in bed was something closer to the reason she read books in the first place. . . . Here was a sign that she wasn't alone.
—ROLAND BARTHES

• • •

When I want to read a good book, I write one.
—BENJAMIN DISRAELI

• • •

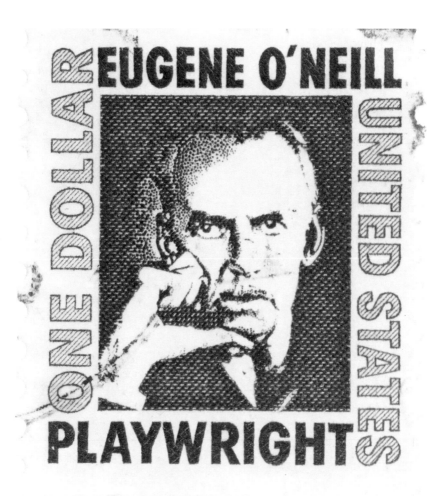

Eugene O'Neil, *Hemera Technologies, PhotoObjects.net, Thinkstock*

I have a good life but I must write because if I do not write a
certain amount I do not enjoy the rest of my life.
—ERNEST HEMINGWAY

• • •

Reading maketh a full man, conference a ready man, and
writing an exact man.
—SIR FRANCIS BACON

• • •

To me, the greatest pleasure of writing is not what it's about,
but the inner music that words make.
—TRUMAN CAPOTE

• • •

My task which I am trying to achieve is, by the power of the
written word, to make you hear, to make you feel—it is, before
all, to make you see. That—and no more, and it is everything.
If I succeed, you shall find there according to your deserts:
encouragement, consolation, fear, charm—all you demand;
and, perhaps, also that glimpse of truth for which you have
forgotten to ask.
—JOSEPH CONRAD

• • •

I shall live badly if I do not write, and I shall write badly if I do not live.
—FRANÇOISE SAGAN

• • •

I hold that a writer who does not passionately believe in the perfectibility of man has no dedication nor any membership in literature.
—JOHN STEINBECK

• • •

It is the writer's privilege to help man endure by lifting his heart.
—WILLIAM FAULKNER

• • •

Words are a writer's tears.
—ARTHUR PLOTNIK

• • •

If a writer is honest, if what is at stake for him can seem to matter to his readers, then his work may be read. But a writer will work anyway, as I do, and as I have, in part to explore this terra incognita, this dangerous ground I seem to need to risk.
—FREDERICK BUSCH

• • •

If you did not write every day, the poisons would accumulate and you would begin to die, or act crazy, or both.
—RAY BRADBURY

• • •

Writing actually empties us and gives us the capacity to love in a completely different way.
—JULIA CAMERON

• • •

You go really deep and connect really large when you write, no matter what you're writing about.
—NATALIE GOLDBERG

• • •

Oscar Wilde, *Photos.com, Thinkstock*

There is no agony like having an untold story inside you.
—TRUMAN CAPOTE

• • •

Of all the inanimate objects, of all men's creations, books are the nearest to us, for they contain our very thoughts, our ambitions, our indignations, our illusions, our fidelity to truth, and our persistent leaning toward error.
—JOSEPH CONRAD

• • •

Writing has so much to give, so much to teach, so many surprises. That thing you had to force yourself to do—the actual act of writing—turns out to be the best part. It's like discovering that while you thought you needed the tea ceremony for the caffeine, what you really needed was the tea ceremony. The act of writing turns out to be its own reward.
—ANNE LAMOTT

• • •

Writing ought either to be the manufacture of stories for which there is a market demand—a business as safe and commendable as making soap or breakfast foods—or it should be an art, which is always a search for something for which there is no market demand, something new and untried, where the values are intrinsic and have nothing to do with standardized values.
—WILLA CATHER

• • •

Out of the artist's imagination, as out of nature's inexhaustible well, pours one thing after another. The artist composes, writes, or paints just as he dreams, seizing whatever swims close to the net. This shimmering mess of loves and hates—fishing trips taken long ago with Uncle Ralph, a 1940 green Chevrolet, a war, a vague sense of what makes a novel, a symphony, a photograph—this is the clay the artist must shape into an object worthy of our attention; that is, our tears, our laughter, our thought.
—JOHN GARDNER

• • •

Writing is so difficult that I feel that writers, having had their hell on earth, will escape all punishment hereafter.
—JESSAMYN WEST

• • •

A writer is a person for whom writing is more difficult than it
is for other people.
—THOMAS MANN

• • •

A strange and mystical business, writing.
—JOHN STEINBECK

• • •

Writing something down often works as a magnet for
other thoughts.
—MARCIA GOLUB

• • •

All good books are alike in that they are truer than if they
had really happened and after you are finished reading one
you will feel that all that happened to you and afterwards
it all belongs to you; the good and the bad, the ecstasy, the
remorse, and sorrow, the people and the places and how the
weather was.
—ERNEST HEMINGWAY

• • •

Like everyone else, I am going to die. But the words–
the words live on for as long as there are readers to
see them, audiences to hear them. It is immortality
by proxy. It is not really a bad deal, all
things considered.
—J. MICHAEL STRACZYNSKI

• • •

Remember that writing is translation, and the opus to be
translated is yourself.
—E. B. WHITE

• • •

In a library we are surrounded by many hundreds of dear
friends imprisoned by an enchanter in paper and
leathern boxes.
—RALPH WALDO EMERSON

• • •

Joseph Conrad, *Photos.com, Thinkstock*

The number one thing I am earnestly attracted to is intelligence. Writers are thus the pinnacle of intelligence. While actors are great and awesome, writers literally create new worlds from scratch. What is sexier than that? Personally, I don't know why every person out there isn't dating a writer.
—RACHEL BLOOM

• • •

I am a galley slave to pen and ink.
—HONORÉ DE BALZAC

• • •

Every word written is a victory against death.
—MICHEL BUTOR

• • •

Better to write for yourself and have no public, than to write for the public and have no self.
—CYRIL CONNOLLY

• • •

For me, writing is exploration; and most of the time, I'm surprised where the journey takes me.
—JACK DANN

• • •

Writing is a cop-out. An excuse to live perpetually in fantasy land, where you can create, direct and watch the products of your own head. Very selfish.
—MONICA DICKENS

• • •

Writing taught my father to pay attention; my father in turn taught other people to pay attention and then write down their thoughts and observations.
—ANNE LAMOTT

• • •

For your born writer, nothing is so healing as the realization that he has come upon the right word.
—CATHERINE DRINKER BOWEN

• • •

Mary Ann Evans ("George Eliot"), *Photos.com, Thinkstock*

The reason one writes isn't the fact he wants to say something.
He writes because he has something to say.
—F. SCOTT FITZGERALD

• • •

Every writer must acknowledge and be able to handle the
unalterable fact that he has, in effect, given
himself a life sentence in solitary confinement.
The ordinary world of work is closed to him—
and that if he's lucky!
—PETER STRAUB

• • •

One wants to tell a story, like Scheherazade, in order not
to die. It's one of the oldest urges of mankind. It's a way of
stalling death.
—CARLOS FUENTES

• • •

Writing wasn't easy to start. After I finally did it, I realized it was the most direct contact possible with the part of myself I thought I had lost, and which I constantly find new things from. Writing also includes the possibility of living many lives as well as living in any time or world possible. I can satisfy my enthusiasm for research, but jump like a calf outside the strict boundaries of science. I can speak about things that are important to me and somebody listens. It's wonderful!
—VIRPI HÄMEEN-ANTTILA

• • •

There is more pleasure to building castles in the air than on the ground.
—EDWARD GIBBON

• • •

We are a species that needs and wants to understand who we are. Sheep lice do not seem to share this longing, which is one reason why they write so little.
—ANNE LAMOTT

• • •

No one is able to enjoy such feast than the one who throws a
party in his own mind.
—SELMA LAGERLÖF

• • •

Are we, who want to create, in some way specially talented
people? Or has everybody else simply given up, either by
pressures of modesty or laziness, and closed their ears from
their inner need to create, until that need has died, forgotten
and abandoned? When you look at children, you start to
think the latter. I still haven't met a child who doesn't love—or
who at least hasn't loved—drawing, writing or some other
creative activity.
—NATALIA LAURILA

• • •

My purpose is to entertain myself first and other
people secondly.
—JOHN D. MACDONALD

• • •

Jean-Jacques Rousseau, *Photos.com, Thinkstock*

Reading usually precedes writing and the impulse to write is almost always fired by reading. Reading, the love of reading, is what makes you dream of becoming a writer.
—SUSAN SONTAG

• • •

If you would not be forgotten as soon as you are dead, either write things worth reading or do things worth writing.
—BENJAMIN FRANKLIN

• • •

The qualities of a second-rate writer can easily be defined, but a first-rate writer can only be experienced. It is just the thing in him which escapes analysis that makes him first-rate.
—WILLA CATHER

• • •

Writing is the only thing that, when I do it, I don't feel I should be doing something else.
—GLORIA STEINEM

• • •

Like everyone else, I am going to die. But the words—the words live on for as long as there are readers to see them, audiences to hear them. It is immortality by proxy. It is not really a bad deal, all things considered.
—J. MICHAEL STRACZYNSKI

• • •

I learned that you should feel when writing, not like Lord Byron on a mountain top, but like a child stringing beads in kindergarten—happy, absorbed and quietly putting one bead on after another.
—BRENDA UELAND

• • •

I can't help but to write, I have a inner need for it. If I'm not in the middle of some literary project, I'm utterly lost, unhappy and distressed. As soon as I get started, I calm down.
—KAARI UTRIO

• • •

If you ask me what I came to do in this world, I, an artist, will
answer you: I am here to live out loud.
—ÉMILE ZOLA

• • •

May I never grow too old to treasure 'once upon a time.'
—ANONYMOUS

• • •

What a writer wants to do is not what he does.
—JORGE LUIS BORGES

• • •

Coleridge was a drug addict. Poe was an alcoholic. Marlowe
was killed by a man whom he was treacherously trying to stab.
Pope took money to keep a woman's name out of a satire then
wrote a piece so that she could still be recognized anyhow.
Chatterton killed himself. Byron was accused of incest. Do
you still want to a writer—and if so, why?
—BENNETT CERF

• • •

Johann Wolfgang von Goethe, *Photos.com, Thinkstock*

Writing is the hardest work in the world. I have been a brick-layer and a truck driver, and I tell you—as if you haven't been told a million times already—that writing is harder. Lonelier. And nobler and more enriching.
—HARLAN ELLISON

• • •

Societies never know it, but the war of an artist with his society is a lover's war, and he does, at his best, what lovers do, which is to reveal the beloved to himself.
—JAMES BALDWIN

• • •

The work never matches the dream of perfection the artist has to start with.
—WILLIAM FAULKNER

• • •

I am irritated by my own writing. I am like a violinist whose ear is true, but whose fingers refuse to reproduce precisely the sound he hears within.
—GUSTAVE FLAUBERT

• • •

Writing is not necessarily something to be ashamed of, but do it in private and wash your hands afterwards.
—ROBERT A. HEINLEIN

• • •

The quality which makes man want to write and be read is essentially a desire for self-exposure and masochism. Like one of those guys who has a compulsion to take his thing out and show it on the street.
—JAMES JONES

• • •

It's tougher than Himalayan yak jerky in January. But, as any creative person will tell you, there are days when there's absolutely nothing sweeter than creating something from nothing.
—RICHARD KRZEMIEN

• • •

All good writing is swimming under water and holding your breath.
—F. SCOTT FITZGERALD

• • •

There is no agony like having an untold story inside you.
—ZORA NEALE HURSTON

• • •

With the passing of years I know that the fate of books is not unlike that of human beings: some bring joy, others anguish. Yet one must resist the urge to throw away pen and paper. After all, authentic writers write even if there is little chance for them to be published; they write because they cannot do otherwise, like Kafka's messenger who is privy to a terrible and imperious truth that no one is willing to receive but is nonetheless compelled to go on.
—ELIE WIESEL

• • •

Writing is not a genteel profession. It's quite nasty and tough and kind of dirty.
—ROSEMARY MAHONEY

• • •

Charles Dickens, *Photos.com, Thinkstock*

All writers are vain, selfish and lazy, and at the very bottom
of their motives lies a mystery. Writing a book is a long,
exhausting struggle, like a long bout of some painful illness.
One would never undertake such a thing if one were not
driven by some demon whom one can neither
resist nor understand.
—GEORGE ORWELL

• • •

If writing seems hard, it's because it is hard. It's one of the
hardest things people do.
—WILLIAM ZINSSER

• • •

Easy reading is damned hard writing.
—ANONYMOUS

• • •

The only thing I was fit for was to be a writer, and this notion
rested solely on my suspicion that I would
never be fit for real work, and that writing didn't
require any.
—RUSSELL BAKER

• • •

You may be able to take a break from writing, but you won't be able to take a break from being a writer.
—STEPHEN LEIGH

• • •

At night, when the objective world has slunk back into its cavern and left dreamers to their own, there come inspirations and capabilities impossible at any less magical and quiet hour. No one knows whether or not he is a writer unless he has tried writing at night.
—H. P. LOVECRAFT

• • •

When once the itch of literature comes over a man, nothing can cure it but the scratching of a pen.
—SAMUEL LOVER

• • •

By speech first, but far more by writing, man has been able to put something of himself beyond death. In tradition and in books an integral part of the individual persists, for it can influence the minds and actions of other people in different places and at different times: a row of black marks on a page can move a man to tears, though the bones of him that wrote it are long ago crumbled to dust.
—JULIAN HUXLEY

• • •

We do not write because we want to; we write because we have to.
—W. SOMERSET MAUGHAM

• • •

One hasn't become a writer until one has distilled writing into a habit, and that habit has been forced into an obsession. Writing has to be an obsession. It has to be something as organic, physiological and psychological as speaking or sleeping or eating.
—NIYI OSUNDARE

• • •

John Rushkin, *Photos.com, Thinkstock*

Through joy and through sorrow, I wrote. Through hunger
and through thirst, I wrote. Through good report and through
ill report, I wrote. Through sunshine and through moonshine,
I wrote. What I wrote it is unnecessary to say.
—EDGAR A. POE

• • •

We tell ourselves stories in order to live.
—JOAN DIDION

• • •

The measure of artistic merit is the length to which a writer is
willing to go in following his own compulsions.
—JOHN UPDIKE

• • •

I never want to see anyone, and I never want to go anywhere
or do anything. I just want to write.
—P. G. WODEHOUSE

• • •

Only those things are beautiful which are inspired by madness
and written by reason.
—ANDRÉ GIDE

• • •

In utter loneliness a writer tries to explain the inexplicable.
—JOHN STEINBECK

• • •

Becoming the reader is the essence of becoming a writer.
—JOHN O'HARA

• • •

Read a lot, finding out what kind of writing turns you on, in
order to develop a criterion for your own writing. And then
trust it—and yourself.
—ROSEMARY DANIELL

• • •

Joseph Addison, *Photos.com, Thinkstock*

Matthew Arnold, *Photos.com, Thinkstock*

The task of a writer consists of being able to make something
out of an idea.
—THOMAS MANN

• • •

Many people hear voices when no one is there. Some of them
are called mad and are shut up in rooms where they stare at
the walls all day. Others are called writers and they do pretty
much the same thing.
—MEG CHITTENDEN

• • •

We are all apprentices in a craft where no one ever
becomes a master.
—ERNEST HEMINGWAY

• • •

Real writers are those who want to write, need to write, have
to write.
—ROBERT PENN WARREN

• • •

To note an artist's limitations is but to define his talent. A reporter can write equally well about everything that is presented to his view, but a creative writer can do his best only with what lies within the range and character of his deepest sympathies.
—WILLA CATHER

• • •

Writing is an exploration. You start from nothing and learn as you go. . . . Writing is like driving at night in the fog. You can only see as far as your headlights, but you can make the whole trip that way. . . . Writing is a socially acceptable form of schizophrenia.
—E. L. DOCTOROW

• • •

Perhaps the critics are right: this generation may not produce literature equal to that of any past generation—who cares? The writer will be dead before anyone can judge him—but he must go on writing, reflecting disorder, defeat, despair, should that be all he sees at the moment, but ever searching for the elusive love, joy, and hope—qualities which, as in the act of life itself, are best when they have to be struggled for, and are not commonly come by with much ease, either by a critic's formula or by a critic's yearning.
—WILLIAM STYRON

• • •

Jules Verne, *Photos.com, Thinkstock*

chapter two

"But What Are They Doing in That Cottage?": How We Write

Have something to say, and say it as clearly as you can. That is the only secret.
—MATTHEW ARNOLD

• • •

However great a man's natural talent may be, the act of writing cannot be learned all at once.
—JEAN-JACQUES ROUSSEAU

• • •

In the most basic way, writers are defined not by the stories they tell, or their politics, or their gender, or their race, but by the words they use. Writing begins with language, and it is in that initial choosing, as one sifts through the wayward lushness of our wonderful mongrel English, that choice of vocabulary and grammar and tone, the selection on the palette, that determines who's sitting at that desk. Language creates the writer's attitude toward the particular story he's decided to tell.
—DONALD E. WESTLAKE

• • •

Don't be 'a writer.' Be writing.
—WILLIAM FAULKNER

• • •

Once the grammar has been learned, writing is simply talking on paper and in time learning what not to say.
—BERYL BAINBRIDGE

• • •

A scrupulous writer, in every sentence that he writes, will ask himself at least four questions, thus: 1. What am I trying to say? 2. What words will express it? 3. What image or idiom will make it clearer? 4. Is this image fresh enough to have an effect?
—GEORGE ORWELL

• • •

Alexandre Dumas the Elder, *Photos.com, Thinkstock*

Oliver Goldsmith, *Photos.com, Thinkstock*

Don't loaf and invite inspiration; light out after it with a club, and if you don't get it you will nonetheless get something that looks remarkably like it.
—JACK LONDON

• • •

The most essential gift for a good writer is a built-in shock-proof shit-detector.
—ERNEST HEMINGWAY

• • •

Writing comes more easily if you have something to say.
—SHOLEM ASCH

• • •

Quantity produces quality. If you only write a few things, you're doomed.
—RAY BRADBURY

• • •

The ear is the only true writer and the only true reader.
—ROBERT FROST

• • •

I believe more in the scissors than I do in the pencil.
—TRUMAN CAPOTE

• • •

I met, not long ago, a young man who aspired to become a novelist. Knowing that I was in the profession, he asked me to tell him how he should set to work to realize his ambition. I did my best to explain. 'The first thing,' I said, 'is to buy quite a lot of paper, a bottle of ink, and a pen. After that you merely have to write.'
—ALDOUS HUXLEY

• • •

Let's get one thing clear right now, shall we? There is no Idea Dump, no Story Central, no Island of the Buried Bestsellers; good story ideas seem to come quite literally from nowhere, sailing at you right out of the empty sky: two previously unrelated ideas come together and make something new under the sun. Your job isn't to find these ideas but to recognize them when they show up.
—STEPHEN KING

• • •

Yes. It's like baking. Writing books is like a combination of writing a song and a letter.
—CARLY SIMON [ANSWERING THE QUESTION, "DOES WRITING A BOOK FEEL THE SAME AS WRITING A SONG?"]

• • •

Mary Wollstonecraft, *Photos.com, Thinkstock*

Sir Arthur Conan Doyle, *Photos.com, Thinkstock*

Increase your word power. Words are the raw material of our craft. The greater your vocabulary the more effective your writing. We who write in English are fortunate to have the richest and most versatile language in the world. Respect it.
—P. D. JAMES

• • •

If you want to be a writer, you have to write every day. The consistency, the monotony, the certainty, all vagaries and passions are covered by this daily reoccurrence. You don't go to a well once but daily. You don't skip a child's breakfast or forget to wake up in the morning. Sleep comes to you each day, and so does the muse.
—WALTER MOSLEY

• • •

You must want to enough. Enough to take all the rejections, enough to pay the price of disappointment and discouragement while you are learning. Like any other artist you must learn your craft—then you can add all the genius you like.
—PHYLLIS A. WHITNEY

• • •

The beautiful part of writing is that you don't have to get it right the first time, unlike, say, brain surgery.
—ROBERT CORMIER

• • •

Murder your darlings. [in the sense that you shouldn't be reluctant to edit yourself]
—SIR ARTHUR QUILLER-COUCH

• • •

There's a good reason why a pencil has an eraser at one end.
—STEVEN D. PRICE

• • •

Prose is like hair, it shines with combing.
—GUSTAVE FLAUBERT

• • •

Close the door. Write with no one looking over your shoulder. Don't try to figure out what other people want to hear from you; figure out what you have to say. It's the one and only thing you have to offer.
—BARBARA KINGSOLVER

• • •

When a man writes from his own mind, he writes very rapidly. The greatest part of a writer's time is spent in reading, in order to write; a man will turn over half a library to make one book.
—SAMUEL JOHNSON

• • •

Émile Zola, *Photos.com, Thinkstock*

Izaak Walton, *Photos.com, Thinkstock*

There is some relationship between the hunger for truth and the search for the right words. This struggle may be ultimately indefinable and even undecidable, but one damn well knows it when one sees it.
—CHRISTOPHER HITCHENS

• • •

A writer needs three things, experience, observation, and imagination, any two of which, at times any one of which, can supply the lack of the others.
—WILLIAM FAULKNER

• • •

Writing makes no noise, except groans, and it can be done everywhere, and it is done alone.
—URSULA K. LE GUIN

• • •

First, there must be talent, much talent. Talent such as Kipling had. Then there must be discipline. The discipline of Flaubert. Then there must be the conception of what it can be and absolute conscience as unchanging as the standard meter in Paris, to prevent faking. Then the writer must be intelligent and disinterested and above all he must survive. Try to get all these in one person and have him come through all the influences that press on a writer. The hardest thing, because time is so short, is for him to survive and get his work done.
—ERNEST HEMINGWAY

• • •

A writer is unfair to himself when he is unable to be hard on himself.
—MARIANNE MOORE

• • •

I was working on the proof of one of my poems all the morning, and took out a comma. In the afternoon I put it back again.
—OSCAR WILDE

• • •

Good writers are those who keep the language efficient. That is to say, keep it accurate, keep it clear.
—EZRA POUND

• • •

Writing a novel is like driving a car at night. You can only see as far as your headlights, but you can make the whole trip that way.
—E. L. DOCTOROW

• • •

Nothing leads so straight to futility as literary ambitions without systematic knowledge.
—H. G. WELLS

• • •

Richard Brinsley Sheridan, *Photos.com, Thinkstock*

Daniel Defoe, *Photos.com, Thinkstock*

Read, read, read. Read everything—trash, classics, good and bad, and see how they do it. Just like a carpenter who works as an apprentice and studies the master. Read! You'll absorb it. Then write. If it's good, you'll find out. If it's not, throw it out of the window.
—WILLIAM FAULKNER

• • •

If you would be a writer, first be a reader. Only through the assimilation of ideas, thoughts and philosophies can one begin to focus his own ideas, thoughts and philosophies.
—ALLAN W. ECKERT

• • •

How do you write? You write, man, you write, that's how, and you do it the way the old English walnut tree puts forth leaf and fruit every year by the thousands. . . . If you practice an art faithfully, it will make you wise, and most writers can use a little wising up.
—WILLIAM SAROYAN

• • •

Write a short story every week. It's not possible to write 52 bad short stories in a row.
—RAY BRADBURY

• • •

If there is a magic in story writing, and I am convinced that there is, no one has ever been able to reduce it to a recipe that can be passed from one person to another. The formula seems to lie solely in the aching urge of the writer to convey something he feels important to the reader. If the writer has that urge, he may sometimes but by no means always find the way to do it.

—JOHN STEINBECK

• • •

A writer—and, I believe, generally all persons—must think that whatever happens to him or her is a resource. All things have been given to us for a purpose, and an artist must feel this more intensely. All that happens to us, including our humiliations, our misfortunes, our embarrassments, all is given to us as raw material, as clay, so that we may shape our art.

—JORGE LUIS BORGES

• • •

You must keep sending work out; you must never let a manuscript do nothing but eat its head off in a drawer. You send that work out again and again, while you're working on another one. If you have talent you'll receive some measure of success—but only if you persist.

—ISAAC ASIMOV

• • •

I write as straight as I can, just as I walk as straight as I can, because that is the best way to get there.

—H. G. WELLS

• • •

Leo Tolstoy, *Photos.com, Thinkstock*

Robert Louis Stevenson, *Photos.com, Thinkstock*

What I like in a good author isn't what he says, but
what he whispers.
—LOGAN PEARSALL SMITH

• • •

At a certain point, while you're failing miserably, you do find
a kind of engine in the book that allows you to move forward
with it. It's a feeling I get when I understand that the thing has
begun to lift off.
—JEFFREY EUGENIDES

• • •

The story is told of Balzac… that one day he found himself
in front of a beautiful picture—a melancholy winter scene,
heavy with hoar frost and thinly sprinkled with collages and
mean-looking peasants; and that after gazing at a little house
from which a thin wisp of smoke was rising, he cried, "How
beautiful it is! But what are they doing in that cottage? What
are their thoughts? What are their sorrows? Has it been a
good harvest? No doubt they have bills to pay!"
—CHARLES BAUDELAIRE

• • •

A line will take us hours maybe; Yet if it does not seem
a moment's thought, our stitching and unstinting has
been naught.
—WILLIAM BUTLER YEATS

• • •

I keep six honest serving men
They taught me all I knew;
Their names are What and Why and When
and How and Where and Who.
—RUDYARD KIPLING

• • •

No one can write decently who is distrustful of the reader's
intelligence or whose attitude is patronizing.
—E. B. WHITE

• • •

Description must work for its place. It can't be simply orna-
mental. It usually works best if it has a human element; it is
more effective if it comes from an implied viewpoint, rather
than from the eye of God. If description is coloured by the viewpoint of the character who is doing the noticing, it becomes, in
effect, part of character definition and part of the action.
—HILARY MANTEL

• • •

When I used to teach creative writing, I would tell the stu-
dents to make their characters want something right away
even if it's only a glass of water. Characters paralyzed by the
meaninglessness of modern life still have to drink water from
time to time.
—KURT VONNEGUT

• • •

Rudyard Kipling, *Photos.com, Thinkstock*

I'm very much aware in the writing of dialogue, or even in the narrative too, of a rhythm. There has to be a rhythm with it … Interviewers have said, you like jazz, don't you? Because we can hear it in your writing. And I thought that was a compliment.
—ELMORE LEONARD

• • •

Don't use words too big for the subject. Don't say 'infinitely' when you mean 'very', otherwise you'll have no word left when you want to talk about something really infinite.
—C. S. LEWIS

• • •

Most of the basic material a writer works with is acquired before the age of fifteen.
—WILLA CATHER

• • •

Writing is just work—there's no secret. If you dictate or use a pen or type or write with your toes—it's still just work.
—SINCLAIR LEWIS

• • •

You can approach the act of writing with nervousness, excitement, hopefulness, or even despair, the sense that you can never completely put on the page what's in your mind and heart. You can come to the act with your fists clenched and

your eyes narrowed, ready to kick ass and take down names. You can come to it because you want a girl to marry you or because you want to change the world. Come to it any way but lightly. Let me say it again: you must not come lightly to the blank page.
—STEPHEN KING

• • •

The best thing to do is to loosen my grip on my pen and let it go wandering about until it finds an entrance. There must be one—everything depends on the circumstances, a rule applicable as much to literary style as to life. Each word tugs another one along, one idea another, and that is how books, governments and revolutions are made—some even say that is how Nature created her species.
—MACHADO DE ASSIS

• • •

A book is like a man—clever and dull, brave and cowardly, beautiful and ugly. For every flowering thought there will be a page like a wet and mangy mongrel, and for every looping flight a tap on the wing and a reminder that wax cannot hold the feathers firm too near the sun… Well—then the book is done. It has no virtue any more. The writer wants to cry out— "Bring it back! Let me rewrite it or better—Let me burn it. Don't let it out in the unfriendly cold in that condition."
—JOHN STEINBECK

• • •

Katherine Mansfield, *Photos.com, Thinkstock*

Everywhere I go, I am asked if I think university stifles writers.
My opinion is that it doesn't stifle enough of them.
—FLANNERY O'CONNOR

• • •

Technique alone is never enough. You have to have passion.
Technique alone is just an embroidered potholder.
—RAYMOND CHANDLER

• • •

When an idea comes, spend silent time with it. Remember
Keats's idea of Negative Capability and Kipling's advice to
"drift, wait and obey". Along with your gathering of hard data,
allow yourself also to dream your idea into being.
—ROSE TREMAIN

• • •

A man may write at any time, if he will set himself doggedly
to it.
—SAMUEL JOHNSON [QUOTED IN BOSWELL:
JOURNAL OF A TOUR TO THE HEBRIDES]

• • •

There are no dull subjects. There are only dull writers.
—H. L. MENCKEN

• • •

In writing a novel, when in doubt, have two guys come
through the door with guns.
—RAYMOND CHANDLER

• • •

What is written without effort is in general read
without pleasure.
—SAMUEL JOHNSON

• • •

Writing is like everything else: the more you do it the better
you get. Don't try to perfect as you go along, just get to the
end of the damn thing. Accept imperfections. Get it finished
and then you can go back. If you try to polish every sentence
there's a chance you'll never get past the first chapter.
—IAIN BANKS

• • •

Neither man nor God is going to tell me what to write.
—JAMES T. FARRELL

• • •

About the most originality that any writer can hope to achieve
honestly is to steal with good judgment.
—JOSH BILLINGS

• • •

When asked, 'How do you write?' I invariably answer, 'one
word at a time.'
—STEPHEN KING

• • •

The secret of getting ahead is getting started.
—AGATHA CHRISTIE

• • •

There is no satisfactory explanation of style, no infallible
guide to good writing, no assurance that a person who thinks
clearly will be able to write clearly, no key that unlocks the
door, no inflexible rules by which the young writer may steer
his course. He will often find himself steering by stars that are
disturbingly in motion.
—E. B. WHITE

• • •

Nothing you write, if you hope to be any good, will ever come
out as you first hoped.
—LILLIAN HELLMAN

• • •

Write something to suit yourself and many people will like it;
write something to suit everybody and scarcely anyone will
care for it.
—JESSE STUART

• • •

Edward Robert Bulwer-Lytton, *Photos.com, Thinkstock*

If you look at anything long enough, say just that wall in front
of you—it will come out of that wall.
—ANTON CHEKOV

• • •

A lot of writing is an acquired schizophrenia. You have to
really allow yourself to be a kind of egomaniac when you
first start a story or a piece of work. Everything you write has
to seem good to you and just get it out. Let it inspire you to
the next sentence and the next scene and the next character.
And in that way, you discover what your story is. But if you're
looking over your own shoulder all the time, crossing every
other sentence out, and holding every other word up to the
light as you're composing, that can lead you to become kind
of constipated as a writer. Later on, you have to look at your
work with a very cold eye, as if you were editing someone
else's. But in that first blush, why not enjoy it?
—TOBIAS WOLFF

• • •

Do give the work a name as quickly as possible. Own it, and
see it. Dickens knew Bleak House was going to be called
Bleak House before he started writing it. The rest must have
been easy.
—RODDY DOYLE

• • •

Write what you know about.
—ERNEST HEMINGWAY

• • •

[John Irving called the above the worst advice for writers that he ever heard: "What a terrible limitation to impose on the novel or the play. 'Don't learn anything'—why don't you just say that?" Irving cited as the best advice for writers Herman Melville's "Woe to him who seeks to please rather than appall."]

• • •

But I always remember Ernest Hemingway's advice to writers: always quit for the day when you know what the next sentence is. If it's coming near the end of a chapter and I'm really getting into it, I tend to get up earlier and earlier, just because I'm excited to get to work.
—ROBERT CARO

• • •

If you write to impress it will always be bad, but if you write to express it will be good.
—THORNTON WILDER

• • •

Whenever you feel an impulse to perpetrate a piece of exceptionally fine writing, obey it—and delete it before sending your manuscript to the press.
—SIR ARTHUR QUILLER-COUCH

• • •

I believe that in a good collaboration, the authors bring their strengths to the story; one author's strength cancels the other author's weakness, and back and forth it goes.
—JACK DANN

• • •

For a creative writer, possession of the "truth" is less important than emotional sincerity.
—GEORGE ORWELL

• • •

To a chemist, nothing on earth is unclean. A writer must be as objective as a chemist; he must abandon the subjective line; he must know that dungheaps play a very respectable part in a landscape, and that evil passions are as inherent in life as good ones.
—ANTON CHEKHOV

• • •

Ideas are like rabbits. You get a couple and learn how to handle them, and pretty soon you have a dozen.
—JOHN STEINBECK

• • •

Don't use adjectives which merely tell us how you want us to feel about the thing you are describing. I mean, instead of telling us a thing was "terrible," describe it so that we'll be

Thomas Hardy, *Photos.com, Thinkstock*

terrified. Don't say it was "delightful"; make us say "delightful" when we've read the description. You see, all those words (horrifying, wonderful, hideous, exquisite) are only like saying to your readers, "Please will you do my job for me."
—C. S. LEWIS

• • •

Don't tell me the moon is shining; show me the glint of light on broken glass.
—ANTON CHEKHOV

• • •

Don't say the old lady screamed. Bring her on and let her scream.
—MARK TWAIN

• • •

Good writing is supposed to evoke sensation in the reader— not the fact that it is raining, but the feeling of being rained upon.
—E. L. DOCTOROW

• • •

Develop craftsmanship through years of wide reading.
—ANNIE PROULX

• • •

The writer learns to write, in the last resort, only by writing. He must get words onto paper even if he is dissatisfied with them. A young writer must cross many psychological barriers to acquire confidence in his capacity to produce good work— especially his first full-length book—and he cannot do this by staring at a piece of blank paper, searching for the perfect sentence.
—PAUL JOHNSON

• • •

Reread, rewrite, reread, rewrite. If it still doesn't work, throw it away. It's a nice feeling, and you don't want to be cluttered with the corpses of poems and stories which have everything in them except the life they need.
—HELEN DUNMORE

• • •

Always try to use the language so as to make quite clear what you mean and make sure your sentence couldn't mean anything else.
—C. S. LEWIS

• • •

Always prefer the plain direct word to the long, vague one. Don't implement promises, but keep them.
—C. S. LEWIS

• • •

Poets need not go to Niagara to write about the force of
falling water.
—ROBERT FROST

• • •

We should not write so that it is possible for the reader to
understand us, but so that it is impossible for him to misun-
derstand us.
—QUINTILIAN (MARCUS FABIUS QUINTILIANUS)

• • •

Never use abstract nouns when concrete ones will do. If you
mean "More people died" don't say "Mortality rose."
—C. S. LEWIS

• • •

You have to know how to accept rejection and
reject acceptance.
—RAY BRADBURY

• • •

No tears in the writer, no tears in the reader. No surprise in
the writer, no surprise in the reader.
—ROBERT FROST

• • •

Jane Austen, *Photos.com, Thinkstock*

Many causes may vitiate a writer's judgement of his own works. On that which has cost him much labour he sets a high value, because he is unwilling to think that he has been diligent in vain: what has been produced without toilsome efforts is considered with delight as a proof of vigorous faculties and fertile invention; and the last work, whatever it be, has necessarily most of the grace of novelty.
—SAMUEL JOHNSON

• • •

Books aren't written—they're rewritten. Including your own. It is one of the hardest things to accept, especially after the seventh rewrite hasn't quite done it.
—MICHAEL CRICHTON

• • •

Nothing leads so straight to futility as literary ambitions without systematic knowledge.
—H. G. WELLS

• • •

The pattern of the thing precedes the thing. I fill in the gaps of the crossword at any spot I happen to choose. These bits I write on index cards until the novel is done. My schedule is flexible, but I am rather particular about my instruments:

lined Bristol cards and well sharpened, not too hard, pencils capped with erasers.
—VLADIMIR NABOKOV

• • •

Only write from your own passion, your own truth. That's the only thing you really know about, and anything else leads you away from the pulse.
—MARIANNE WILLIAMSON

• • •

A story needs rhythm. Read it aloud to yourself. If it doesn't spin a bit of magic, it's missing something.
—ESTHER FREUD

• • •

The way you define yourself as a writer is that you write every time you have a free minute. If you didn't behave that way you would never do anything.
—JOHN IRVING

• • •

Writing is physical work. It's sweaty work. You just can't will yourself to become a good writer. You really have to work at it.
—WILL HAYGOOD

• • •

Fill your paper with the breathings of your heart.
—WILLIAM WORDSWORTH

• • •

James Matthew Barrie, *Photos.com, Thinkstock*

Charlotte Bronte, *Photos.com, Thinkstock*

You can't say, I won't write today because that excuse will extend into several days, then several months, then… you are not a writer anymore, just someone who dreams about being a writer.
—DOROTHY C. FONTANA

• • •

A writer never has a vacation. For a writer life consists of either writing or thinking about writing.
—EUGÈNE IONESCO

• • •

What I try to do with myself is just avoid the success or failure thing. Because there is so much about writing that is out of the writer's control. Not the action of doing it, but whether it comes alive or not. If I begin thinking in terms of failure, what happens is I get really depressed, and the game is over, because I've already decided.
—DAVID FOSTER WALLACE

• • •

No, it's not a very good story—its author was too busy listening to other voices to listen as closely as he should have to the one coming from inside.
—STEPHEN KING

• • •

Put it before them briefly so they will read it, clearly so they will appreciate it, picturesquely so they will remember it, and above all, accurately so they will be guided by its light.
—JOSEPH PULITZER

• • •

Start early and work hard. A writer's apprenticeship usually involves writing a million words (which are then discarded) before he's almost ready to begin. That takes a while.
—DAVID EDDINGS

• • •

To imagine yourself inside another person . . . is what a story writer does in every piece of work; it is his first step, and his last too, I suppose.
—EUDORA WELTY

• • •

I took a number of stories by popular writers as well as others by Maupassant, O. Henry, Stevenson, etc., and studied them carefully. Modifying what I learned over the next few years, I began to sell.
—LOUIS L'AMOUR

• • •

Beginning writers must appreciate the prerequisites if they hope to become writers. You pay your dues—which takes years."
—ALEX HALEY

• • •

Edgar Allan Poe, *Photos.com, Thinkstock*

Hans Christian Andersen, *Photos.com, Thinkstock*

Only ambitious nonentities and hearty mediocrities exhibit their rough drafts. It's like passing around samples of sputum.
—VLADIMIR NABOKOV

• • •

Writing energy is like anything else. The more you put in, the more you get out.
—RICHARD REEVES

• • •

Exercise the writing muscle every day, even if it is only a letter, notes, a title list, a character sketch, a journal entry. Writers are like dancers, like athletes. Without that exercise, the muscles seize up.
—JANE YOLEN

• • •

Like stones, words are laborious and unforgiving, and the fitting of them together, like the fitting of stones, demands great patience and strength of purpose and particular skill.
—EDMUND MORRISON

• • •

People on the outside think there's something magical about writing, that you go up in the attic at midnight and cast the bones and come down in the morning with a story, but it isn't like that. You sit in back of the typewriter and you work, and that's all there is to it.
—HARLAN ELLISON

• • •

My aim is to put down on paper what I see and what I feel in the best and simplest way.
—ERNEST HEMINGWAY

• • •

Our admiration of fine writing will always be in proportion to its real difficulty and its apparent ease.
—CHARLES CALEB COLTON

• • •

Even in literature and art, no man who bothers about originality will ever be original: whereas if you simply try to tell the truth (without caring twopence how often it has been told before) you will, nine times out of ten, become original without ever having noticed it.
—C. S. LEWIS

• • •

The muse whispers to you when she chooses, and you can't tell her to come back later, because you quickly learn in this business that she might not come back at all.
—TERRY BROOKS

• • •

The author must keep his mouth shut when his work starts to speak.
—FRIEDRICH NIETZSCHE

• • •

James Boswell, *Photos.com, Thinkstock*

Petrarch, *iStockphoto, Thinkstock*

Don't romanticise your "vocation". You can either write good sentences or you can't. There is no "writer's lifestyle". All that matters is what you leave on the page.
—ZADIE SMITH

• • •

Hardly anybody ever writes anything nice about introverts. Extroverts rule. This is rather odd when you realize that about nineteen writers out of twenty are introverts. We have been taught to be ashamed of not being 'outgoing'. But a writer's job is ingoing.
—URSULA K. LE GUIN

• • •

There is no way of writing well and also of writing easily.
—ANTHONY TROLLOPE

• • •

To be a writer is to sit down at one's desk in the chill portion of every day, and to write; not waiting for the little jet of the blue flame of genius to start from the breastbone—just plain going at it, in pain and delight. To be a writer is to throw away a great deal, not to be satisfied, to type again, and then again, and once more, and over and over. . . .
—JOHN HERSEY

• • •

The mark of a really great writer is that he gives expression to what the masses of mankind think or feel without knowing it. The mediocre writer simply writes what everyone would have said.
—G. C. LICHTENBERG

• • •

The faster I write the better my output. If I'm going slow, I'm in trouble. It means I'm pushing the words instead of being pulled by them.
—RAYMOND CHANDLER

• • •

When we read, we start at the beginning and continue until we reach the end. When we write, we start in the middle and fight our way out.
—VICKIE KARP

• • •

The heart makes the eloquence.
—EDWARD DAHLBERG

• • •

A classic is classic not because it conforms to certain structural rules, or fits certain definitions (of which its author had quite probably never heard). It is classic because of a certain eternal and irrepressible freshness.
—EDITH WHARTON

• • •

William Cullen Bryant, *iStockphoto, Thinkstock*

Robert Browning, *iStockphoto, Thinkstock*

Many remarkable writers not only survive immense amounts
of hack work, they gain know-how from it.
—CHRISTOPHER ISHERWOOD

• • •

If you want to be a writer, you must do two things above all
others: read a lot and write a lot.
—STEPHEN KING

• • •

Only that which does not teach, which does not cry out,
which does not condescend, which does not explain,
is irresistible.
—WILLIAM BUTLER YEATS

• • •

In utter loneliness a writer tries to explain the inexplicable.
And sometimes if he is very fortunate and if the time is right,
a very little of what he is trying to do trickles through—not
ever much. And if he is a writer wise enough to know it can't
be done, then he is not a writer at all. A good writer always
works at the impossible. There is another kind who pulls
in his horizons, drops his mind as one lowers rifle sights.
And giving up the impossible he gives up writing. Whether
fortunate or unfortunate, this has not happened to me. The
same blind effort, the straining, and puffing go on in me. And
always I hope that a little trickles through. This urge dies hard.
—JOHN STEINBECK

• • •

Forget all the rules. Forget about being published. Write for yourself and celebrate writing.
—MELINDA HAYNES

• • •

Close the door. Write with no one looking over your shoulder. Don't try to figure out what other people want to hear from you; figure out what you have to say. It's the one and only thing you have to offer.
—BARBARA KINGSOLVER

• • •

I don't think it is possible to give tips for finding one's voice; it's one of those things for which there aren't really any tricks or shortcuts, or even any advice that necessarily translates from writer to writer. All I can tell you is to write as much as possible.
—POPPY Z. BRITE

• • •

If the doctor told me I had six minutes to live, I'd type a little faster.
—ISAAC ASIMOV

• • •

William Shakespeare, *Hemera,* *Thinkstock*

Geoffrey Chaucer, *Hemera,* *Thinkstock*

Never save anything for your next book, because that possible creation may not be properly shaped to hold the thoughts you're working with today. In fiction especially, anything that could happen, should happen.
—TAM MOSSMAN

• • •

You most likely need a thesaurus, a rudimentary grammar book, and a grip on reality. This latter means: there's no free lunch. Writing is work. It's also gambling. You don't get a pension plan. Other people can help you a bit, but essentially you're on your own.
Nobody is making you do this: you chose it, so don't whine.
—MARGARET ATWOOD

• • •

Success is a finished book, a stack of pages each of which is filled with words. If you reach that point, you have won a victory over yourself no less impressive than sailing single-handed around the world.
—TOM CLANCY

• • •

Don't panic. Midway through writing a novel, I have regularly experienced moments of bowel-curdling terror, as I contemplate the drivel on the screen before me and see beyond it, in quick succession, the derisive reviews, the friends' embarrassment, the failing career, the dwindling income, the repossessed house, the divorce . . . Working doggedly on through crises like these, however, has always got me there in the end. Leaving the desk for a while can help. Talking the problem through can help me recall what I was trying to achieve before I got stuck. Going for a long walk almost always gets me thinking about my manuscript in a slightly new way. And if all else fails, there's prayer. St Francis de Sales, the patron saint of writers, has often helped me out in a crisis. If you want to spread your net more widely, you could try appealing to Calliope, the muse of epic poetry, too.

—SARAH WATERS

• • •

Ben Jonson, *Hemera,* *Thinkstock*

Benjamin Franklin, *Hemera,* *Thinkstock*

chapter three

"Show Me the Glint of Light": Writing Fiction

There are three rules for writing the novel. Unfortunately, no one knows what they are.
—W. SOMERSET MAUGHAM

• • •

I am a man, and alive. . . . For this reason I am a novelist. And being a novelist, I consider myself superior to the saint, the scientist, the philosopher, and the poet, who are all great masters of different bits of man alive, but never get the whole hog.
—D. H. LAWRENCE

• • •

Voltaire, *Hemera, Thinkstock*

The acceptance that all that is solid has melted into the air, that reality and morality are not givens but imperfect human constructs, is the point from which fiction begins.
—SALMAN RUSHDIE

• • •

The good ended happily, and the bad unhappily. That is what fiction means.
—OSCAR WILDE

• • •

There are some subjects that can only be tackled in fiction.
—JOHN LE CARRÈ

• • •

Why shouldn't truth be stranger than fiction? Fiction, after all, has to make sense.
—MARK TWAIN

• • •

The main question to a novel is—did it amuse? were you surprised at dinner coming so soon? did you mistake eleven for ten? were you too late to dress? and did you sit up beyond the usual hour? If a novel produces these effects, it is good; if it does not—story, language, love, scandal itself cannot save it. It is only meant to please; and it must do that or it does nothing.
—SYDNEY SMITH

• • •

Alexander Pope, *Hemera, Thinkstock*

The difference between reality and fiction? Fiction has to make sense.
—TOM CLANCY

• • •

Fiction writers are strange beasts. They are, like all writers, observers first and foremost. Everything that happens to and around them is potential material for a story, and they look at it that way.
—TERRY BROOKS

• • •

The first thing you have to consider when writing a novel is your story, and then your story—and then your story!
—FORD MADOX FORD

• • •

No one says a novel has to be one thing. It can be anything it wants to be, a vaudeville show, the six o'clock news, the mumblings of wild men saddled by demons.
—ISHMAEL REED

• • •

Fiction reveals truth that reality obscures.
—RALPH WALDO EMERSON

• • •

The novel is the one bright book of life. Books are not life. They are only tremulations on the ether. But the novel as a tremulation can make the whole man alive tremble.
—D. H. LAWRENCE

• • •

Fiction is more interesting than any other form of literature, to those who really like to study people, is that in fiction the author can really tell the truth without humiliating himself.
—JIM ROHN

• • •

Fiction that isn't an author's personal adventure into the frightening or the unknown isn't worth writing for anything but money.
—JONATHAN FRANZEN

• • •

A novel is never anything but a philosophy put into images.
—ALBERT CAMUS

• • •

One can be absolutely truthful and sincere even though admittedly the most outrageous liar. Fiction and invention are of the very fabric of life.
—HENRY MILLER

• • •

René Descartes, *Hemera,* *Thinkstock*

Michel de Montaigne, *Hemera,* *Thinkstock*

Literature is a luxury; fiction is a necessity.
—GILBERT K. CHESTERTON

• • •

A woman must have money and a room of her own if she is to write fiction.
—VIRGINIA WOOLF

• • •

Fiction is to the grown man what play is to the child; it is there that he changes the atmosphere and tenor of his life.
—ROBERT LOUIS STEVENSON

• • •

Respect the way characters may change once they've got 50 pages of life in them. Revisit your plan at this stage and see whether certain things have to be altered to take account of these changes.
—ROSE TREMAIN

• • •

Short stories are designed to deliver their impact in as few pages as possible. A tremendous amount is left out, and a good short story writer learns to include only the most essential information.
—ORSON SCOTT CARD

• • •

The stupidity of people comes from having an answer for everything. The wisdom of the novel comes from having a question for everything. . . . The novelist teaches the reader to comprehend the world as a question. There is wisdom and tolerance in that attitude. In a world built on sacrosanct certainties the novel is dead. The totalitarian world, whether founded on Marx, Islam, or anything else, is a world of answers rather than questions. There, the novel has no place.
—MILAN KUNDERA

• • •

A short story is a love affair, a novel is a marriage. A short story is a photograph; a novel is a film.
—LORRIE MOORE

• • •

It means that no matter what you write, be it a biography, an autobiography, a detective novel, or a conversation on the street, it all becomes fiction as soon as you write it down.
—GUILLERMO CABRERA INFANTE

• • •

Fiction is the truth inside the lie.
—STEPHEN KING

• • •

William Wordsworth, *iStockphoto, Thinkstock*

Walter Scott, *iStockphoto, Thinkstock*

Science fiction writers foresee the inevitable, and although problems and catastrophes may be inevitable, solutions are not.
—ISAAC ASIMOV

• • •

I just think that fiction that isn't exploring what it means to be human today isn't art.
—DAVID FOSTER WALLACE

• • •

Fiction was invented the day Jonah arrived home and told his wife that he was three days late because he had been swallowed by a whale.
—GABRIEL GARCÍA MÁRQUEZ

• • •

People wonder why the novel is the most popular form of literature; people wonder why it is read more than books of science or books of metaphysics. The reason is very simple; it is merely that the novel is more true than they are.
—G. K. CHESTERTON

• • •

Writing fiction is not "self-expression" or "therapy". Novels are for readers, and writing them means the crafty, patient, selfless construction of effects. I think of my novels as being something like fairground rides: my job is to strap the reader into their car at the start of chapter one, then trundle and whiz them through scenes and surprises, on a carefully planned route, and at a finely engineered pace.
—SARAH WATERS

• • •

Truth is so hard to tell, it sometimes needs fiction to make it plausible.
—SIR FRANCIS BACON

• • •

Everything a writer learns about the art or craft of fiction takes just a little away from his need or desire to write at all. In the end he knows all the tricks and has nothing to say.
—RAYMOND CHANDLER

• • •

Noah Webster, *iStockphoto, Thinkstock*

Sir Francis Bacon, *iStockphoto, Thinkstock*

Concentrate your narrative energy on the point of change. This is especially important for historical fiction. When your character is new to a place, or things alter around them, that's the point to step back and fill in the details of their world. People don't notice their everyday surroundings and daily routine, so when writers describe them it can sound as if they're trying too hard to instruct the reader.
—HILARY MANTEL

• • •

Fiction is like a spider's web, attached ever so slightly perhaps, but still attached to life at all four corners. Often the attachment is scarcely perceptible.
—VIRGINIA WOOLF

• • •

Two hours of writing fiction leaves this writer completely drained. For those two hours he has been in a different place with totally different people.
—ROALD DAHL

• • •

Writing fiction is for me a fraught business, an occasion of daily dread for at least the first half of the novel, and sometimes all the way through. The work process is totally different from writing nonfiction. You have to sit down every day and make it up.
—JOAN DIDION

• • •

And really the purpose of art—for me, fiction—is to alert, to indicate to stop, to say: Make certain that when you rush through you will not miss the moment which you might have had, or might still have.
—JERZY KOSIŃSKI

• • •

Novels for me are how I find out what's going on in my own head. And so that's a really useful and indeed critical thing to do when you do as many of these other things as I do.
—CORY DOCTOROW

• • •

Every writer knows he is spurious; every fiction writer would rather be credible than authentic.
—JOHN LE CARRÉ

• • •

Each book, intuitively sensed and, in the case of fiction, intuitively worked out, stands on what has gone before, and grows out of it. I feel that at any stage of my literary career it could have been said that the last book contained all the others.
—V. S. NAIPAUL

• • •

An unread story is not a story; it is little black marks on wood pulp. The reader, reading it, makes it live: a live thing, a story.
—URSULA K. LE GUIN

• • •

Story is to human beings what the pearl is to the oyster.
—JOSEPH GOLD

• • •

When writing a novel a writer should create living people; people not characters. A character is a caricature.
—ERNEST HEMINGWAY

• • •

It's with bad sentiments that one makes good novels.
—ALDOUS HUXLEY

• • •

Washington Irving, *iStockphoto, Thinkstock*

The only reason for the existence of a novel is that it does
attempt to represent life.
—HENRY JAMES

• • •

Would you not like to try all sorts of lives—one is so very
small—but that is the satisfaction of writing—one can impersonate so many people.
—KATHERINE MANSFIELD

• • •

For if the proper study of mankind is man, it is evidently more
sensible to occupy yourself with the coherent, substantial and
significant creatures of fiction than with the irrational and
shadowy figures of real life.
—W. SOMERSET MAUGHAM

• • •

The novel does not seek to establish a privileged language but
it insists upon the freedom to portray and analyze the struggle
between the different contestants for such privileges.
—SALMAN RUSHDIE

• • •

A writer of fiction lives in fear. Each new day demands new ideas and he can never be sure whether he is going to come up with them or not.
—ROALD DAHL

• • •

It is only a novel . . . or, in short, only some work in which the greatest powers of the mind are displayed, in which the most thorough knowledge of human nature, the happiest delineation of its varieties, the liveliest effusions of wit and humour, are conveyed to the world in the best-chosen language.
—JANE AUSTEN

• • •

If you write fiction you are, in a sense, corrupted. There's a tremendous corruptibility for the fiction writer because you're dealing mainly with sex and violence. These remain the basic themes, they're the basic themes of Shakespeare whether you like it or not.
—ANTHONY BURGESS

• • •

I like shape very much. A novel has to have shape, and life
doesn't have any.
—JEAN RHYS

• • •

But the total, absorbed experience of a novel actually removes
us from the tyranny of our sense of time. It's like a little life
within life, obeying its own permissive laws
of narrative physics.
—GRAHAM SWIFT

• • •

But I hate things all fiction . . . there should always be some
foundation of fact for the most airy fabric—and pure invention is but the talent of a liar.
—LORD BYRON

• • •

What is a novel if not a conviction of our fellow-men's existence strong enough to take upon itself a form of imagined life
clearer than reality and whose accumulated verisimilitude of
selected episodes puts to shame the pride of
documentary history?
—JOSEPH CONRAD

• • •

I at least have so much to do in unraveling certain human lots, and seeing how they were woven and interwoven, that all the light I can command must be concentrated on this particular web, and not dispersed over that tempting range of relevancies called the universe.
—GEORGE ELIOT

• • •

A good novel is like a welcome pause in the flow of our existence; a great novel is forever revisitable. Novels can linger with us long after we've read them—even, and perhaps particularly, novels that compel us to read them, all other concerns forgotten, in a single intense sitting. We may sometimes count pages as we read, but I don't think we look at our watches to see how time is slipping away.
—GRAHAM SWIFT

• • •

Writing a novel is not merely going on a shopping expedition across the border to an unreal land: it is hours and years spent in the factories, the streets, the cathedrals of the imagination.
—JANET FRAME

• • •

The house of fiction:—has in short not one window but a million—a number of possible windows not to be reckoned, rather; every one of which has been pierced, or is still pierce-able in its vast front, by the need of the individual vision and by the pressure of the individual will. These apertures of dissimilar shape and size hang so, altogether, over the human scene that we might expect of them a greater sameness of report than we find. They are but windows at the best, mere holes in a dead wall, disconnected . . . they are but windows at they are not hinged doors opening straight upon life. But they have this mark of their own that at each of them stands a figure with a pair of eyes, or at least with a field-glass, which forms, again and again, for observation, a unique instrument, insuring to the person making use of it as impression distinct from every other. He and his neighbors are watching the same show, but one seeing more where the other sees less, one seeing black where the other sees white, one seeing big where the other sees small and so on . . .

—HENRY JAMES

• • •

Lord Byron, *iStockphoto, Thinkstock*

chapter four

ॐ

"As One Who Carries the Light Bulb": Writing Poetry

A poem begins with a lump in the throat.
—ROBERT FROST

• • •

Poetry is what in a poem makes you laugh, cry, prickle, be
silent, makes your toe nails twinkle, makes you want to do
this or that or nothing, makes you know that you are alone in
the unknown world, that your bliss and suffering is forever
shared and forever all your own.
—DYLAN THOMAS

• • •

Poetry makes nothing happen/It survives in the valley of its saying.
—MAXINE KUMIN

• • •

Poetry is the journal of the sea animal living on land, wanting to fly in the air. Poetry is a search for syllables to shoot at the barriers of the unknown and the unknowable. Poetry is a phantom script telling how rainbows are made and why they go away.
—CARL SANDBURG

• • •

A lot of being a poet consists of willed ignorance. If you woke up from your trance and realized the nature of the life-threatening and dignity-destroying precipice you were walking along, you would switch into actuarial sciences immediately.
—MARGARET ATWOOD

• • •

I wish our clever young poets would remember my homely definitions of prose and poetry; that is prose; words in their best order;—poetry; the best words in the best order.
—SAMUEL TAYLOR COLERIDGE

• • •

John Keats, *iStockphoto, Thinkstock*

Edmund Spenser, *iStockphoto, Thinkstock*

A good poet is someone who manages, in a lifetime of standing out in thunderstorms, to be struck by lightening five or six times; a dozen or two dozen times and he is great.
—RANDALL JARRELL

• • •

Immature poets imitate; mature poets steal.
—T. S. ELIOT

• • •

All slang is a metaphor, and all metaphor is poetry.
—G. K. CHESTERON

• • •

I believe that every English poet should read the English classics, master the rules of grammar before he attempts to bend or break them, travel abroad, experience the horrors of sordid passion, and—if he is lucky enough—know the love of an honest woman.
—ROBERT GRAVES

• • •

My poems are hymns of praise to the glory of life.
—EDITH SITWELL

• • •

Great poetry is always written by somebody straining to go beyond what he can do.
—STEPHEN SPENDER

• • •

A poem is true if it hangs together. Information points to something else. A poem points to nothing but itself.
—E. M. FORSTER

• • •

Poetry should please by a fine excess and not by singularity. It should strike the reader as a wording of his own highest thoughts, and appear almost as a remembrance.
—JOHN KEATS

• • •

Poets don't draw. They unravel their handwriting and then tie it up again, but differently.
—JEAN COCTEAU

• • •

Even when poetry has a meaning, as it usually has, it may be inadvisable to draw it out. . . . Perfect understanding will sometimes almost extinguish pleasure.
—A. E. HOUSMAN

• • •

Victor Hugo, *iStockphoto, Thinkstock*

Miguel de Cervantes Saavedra, *iStockphoto, Thinkstock*

It is always hard for poets to believe that one says their poems
are bad not because one is a fiend but because their
poems are bad.
—RANDALL JARRELL

• • •

A poet ought not to pick nature's pocket. Let him borrow, and
so borrow as to repay by the very act of borrowing. Examine
nature accurately, but write from recollection, and trust more
to the imagination than the memory.
—SAMUEL TAYLOR COLERIDGE

• • •

A poem is never finished, only abandoned.
—PAUL VALÉRY

• • •

Words too familiar, or too remote, defeat the purpose of a
poet. From those sounds which we hear on small or on coarse
occasions, we do not easily receive strong impressions, or
delightful images; and words to which we are nearly strangers,
whenever they occur, draw that attention on themselves which
they should transmit to other things.
—SAMUEL JOHNSON

• • •

Everybody has their own idea of what's a poet. Robert Frost, President Johnson, T. S. Eliot, Rudolf Valentino—they're all poets. I like to think of myself as the one who carries the light bulb.
—BOB DYLAN

• • •

Poetry is not a turning loose of emotion, but an escape from emotion; it is not the expression of personality, but an escape from personality. But, of course, only those who have personality and emotions know what it means to want to escape from these things.
—T. S. ELIOT

• • •

Poetry is just the evidence of life. If your life is burning well, poetry is just the ash.
—LEONARD COHEN

• • •

Poetry is a deal of joy and pain and wonder, with a dash of the dictionary.
—KAHLIL GIBRAN

• • •

Poetry is what gets lost in translation.
—ROBERT FROST

• • •

Jonathan Swift, *iStockphoto, Thinkstock*

Dante Alighieri, *iStockphoto, Thinkstock*

[Poetry is] Imaginary gardens with real toads in them.
—MARIANNE MOORE

• • •

Most people ignore most poetry because most poetry ignores
most people.
—ADRIAN MITCHELL

• • •

Every English poet should master the rules of grammar before
he attempts to bend or break them.
—ROBERT GRAVES

• • •

No man can read Hardy's poems collected but that his own
life, and forgotten moments of it, will come back to him, in a
flash here and an hour there. Have you a better test
of true poetry?
—EZRA POUND

• • •

Publishing a volume of verse is like dropping a rose-petal
down the Grand Canyon and waiting for the echo.
—DON MARQUIS

• • •

In my view a good poem is one in which the form of the
verse and the joining of its parts seems light as a shallow river
flowing over its sandy bed.
—BASHO

• • •

Use no superfluous word, no adjective, which does not reveal
something. Don't use such an expression as 'dim land of
peace.' It dulls the image. It mixes an abstraction with the concrete. It comes from the writer's not realizing that the natural
object is always the adequate symbol. Go in
fear of abstractions.
—EZRA POUND

• • •

A poet's hope: to be,
like some valley cheese,
local, but prized elsewhere.
—W. H. AUDEN

• • •

Poetry is simply the most beautiful, impressive, and widely
effective mode of saying things, and hence its importance.
—MATTHEW ARNOLD

• • •

Samuel Taylor Coleridge, *iStockphoto, Thinkstock*

Andrew Marvell, *iStockphoto, Thinkstock*

Poetry fettered fetters the human race.
—WILLIAM BLAKE

• • •

To break the pentameter, that was the first heave.
—EZRA POUND

• • •

I consider myself a poet first and a musician second. I live like
a poet and I'll die like a poet.
—BOB DYLAN

• • •

I have never started a poem yet whose end I knew. Writing a
poem is discovering.
—ROBERT FROST

• • •

The poet is the priest of the invisible.
—WALLACE STEVENS

• • •

Poetry is, at bottom, a criticism of life.
—MATTHEW ARNOLD

• • •

The poet's mind is in fact a receptacle for seizing and storing up numberless feelings, phrases, images, which remain there until all the particles which can unite to form a new compound are present together.
—T. S. ELIOT

• • •

As a guiding principle I believe that every poem must be its own sole freshly-created universe, and therefore have no belief in 'tradition' or a common myth-kitty or casual allusions in poems to other poems or poets, which last I find unpleasantly like the talk of literary understrappers letting you see they know the right people.
—PHILIP LARKIN

• • •

I think a poet is anybody who wouldn't call himself a poet.
—BOB DYLAN

• • •

I could no more define poetry than a terrier can define a rat.
—A. E. HOUSMAN

• • •

If I feel physically as if the top of my head were taken off, I know that is poetry.
—EMILY DICKINSON

• • •

William Cowper, *iStockphoto, Thinkstock*

There are three things, after all, that a poem must reach: the eye, the ear, and what we may call the heart or the mind. It is most important of all to reach the heart of the reader.
—ROBERT FROST

• • •

Modesty is a virtue not often found among poets, for almost every one of them thinks himself the greatest in the world.
—MIGUEL DE CERVANTES

• • •

He who draws noble delights from sentiments of poetry is a true poet, though he has never written a line in all his life.
—GEORGE SAND

• • •

Always be a poet, even in prose.
—CHARLES BAUDELAIRE

• • •

Poetry is a mirror which makes beautiful that which is distorted.
—PERCY BYSSHE SHELLEY

• • •

Poetry is nearer to vital truth than history.
—PLATO

• • •

It is absurd to think that the only way to tell if a poem is lasting is to wait and see if it lasts. The right reader of a good poem can tell the moment it strikes him that he has taken an immortal wound—that he will never get over it.
—ROBERT FROST

• • •

Out of the quarrel with others we make rhetoric; out of the quarrel with ourselves we make poetry.
—WILLIAM BUTLER YEATS

• • •

Poetry is a packsack of invisible keepsakes.
—CARL SANDBURG

• • •

Poetry should . . . should strike the reader as a wording of his own highest thoughts, and appear almost a remembrance.
—JOHN KEATS

• • •

John Dryden, *iStockphoto, Thinkstock*

To see the Summer Sky Is Poetry, though never in a Book it lie—True Poems flee.
—EMILY DICKINSON

• • •

The poet is in the end probably more afraid of the dogmatist who wants to extract the message from the poem and throw the poem away than he is of the sentimentalist who says, "Oh, just let me enjoy the poem."
—ROBERT PENN WARREN

• • •

Poets are the unacknowledged legislators of the world.
—PERCY BYSSHE SHELLEY

• • •

Being a poet is one of the unhealthier jobs—no regular hours, so many temptations!
—ELIZABETH BISHOP

• • •

A prose writer gets tired of writing prose, and wants to be a poet. So he begins every line with a capital letter, and keeps on writing prose.
—SAMUEL MCCHORD CROTHERS

• • •

Poetry is man's rebellion against being what he is.
—JAMES BRANCH CABELL

• • •

A poet is an unhappy being whose heart is torn by secret sufferings, but whose lips are so strangely formed that when the sighs and the cries escape them, they sound like beautiful music . . . and then people crowd about the poet and say to him: "Sing for us soon again;" that is as much as to say, May new sufferings torment your soul.
—SØREN KIERKEGAARD

• • •

It is the job of poetry to clean up our word-clogged reality by creating silences around things.
—STÉPHENE MALLARMÉ

• • •

The true poet is all the time a visionary and whether with friends or not, as much alone as a man on his deathbed.
—W. B. YEATS

• • •

There is poetry as soon as we realize that we possess nothing.
—JOHN CAGE

• • •

Poetry is the language in which man explores his
own amazement.
—CHRISTOPHER FRY

• • •

If Galileo had said in verse that the world moved, the inquisi-
tion might have let him alone.
—THOMAS HARDY

• • •

All a poet can do is warn.
—WILFRED OWEN

• • •

Poetry creates the myth, the prose writer draws its portrait.
—JEAN-PAUL SARTRE

• • •

And as to experience—well, think how little some good poets have had, or how much some bad ones have.
—ELIZABETH BISHOP

• • •

Poets are interested mostly in death and commas.
—CAROLYN KIZER

• • •

Poets are the hierophants of an unapprehended inspiration; the mirrors of the gigantic shadows which futurity casts upon the present; the words which express what they understand not; the trumpets which sing to battle, and feel not what they inspire; the influence which is moved not, but moves. Poets are the unacknowledged legislators of the world.
—PERCY BYSSHE SHELLEY

• • •

Homer, *iStockphoto, Thinkstock*

Frances Milton Trollope, *iStockphoto, Thinkstock*

chapter five

"They Ripen with Keeping": Letter Writing

The word that is heard perishes, but the letter that is
written remains.
—LATIN PROVERB

• • •

In an age like ours, which is not given to letter-writing, we
forget what an important part it used to play in people's lives.
—ANATOLE BROYARD

• • •

A person who can write a long letter with ease, cannot write ill.
—JANE AUSTEN

• • •

Letters to absence can a voice impart/And lend a tongue when distance gags the heart.
—HORACE WALPOLE

• • •

Letter writing is an excellent way of slowing down this lunatic helterskelter universe long enough to gather one's thoughts.
—NICK BANTOCK

• • •

Letters are like wine; if they are sound they ripen with keeping. A man should lay down letters as he does a cellar of wine.
—SAMUEL BUTLER

• • •

To send a letter is a good way to go somewhere without
moving anything but your heart.
—PHYLLIS THEROUX

• • •

In a man's letters you know, Madam, his soul lies naked, his letters are only the mirror of his breast, whatever passes within him
is shown undisguised in its natural process. Nothing is inverted,
nothing distorted, you see systems in their elements, you discover actions in their motives.
—SAMUEL JOHNSON

• • •

When he wrote a letter, he would put that which was most
material in the postscript, as if it had been a by-matter.
— SIR FRANCIS BACON

• • •

One of the pleasures of reading old letters is the knowledge
that they need no answer.
—LORD BYRON

• • •

Correspondences are like small clothes before the invention of suspenders; it is impossible to keep them up.
—SYDNEY SMITH

• • •

In the midst of great joy do not promise to give a man anything; in the midst of great anger do not answer a man's letter.
—CHINESE PROVERB

• • •

It takes two to write a letter as much as it takes two to make a quarrel.
—ELIZABETH DREW

• • •

If you write one story, it may be bad; if you write a hundred, you have the odds in your favor.
—EDGAR RICE BURROUGHS

• • •

You don't know a woman until you have a letter from her.
—ADA LEVERSON

• • •

To find out your real opinion of someone, judge the impression you have when you first see a letter from them.
—ARTHUR SCHOPENHAUER

• • •

If you are in doubt whether to write a letter or not, don't. And the advice applies to many doubts in life besides that of letter writing.
—EDWARD BULWER-LYTTON

• • •

The best time to frame an answer to the letters of a friend, is the moment you receive them. Then the warmth of friendship, and the intelligence received, most forcibly cooperate.
—WILLIAM SHENSTONE

• • •

Letter writing is the only device for combining solitude with good company.
—LORD BYRON

• • •

One good thing about not seeing you is that I can write you letters.
—SVETLANA ALLILUYEVA

• • •

Letters have to pass two tests before they can be classed as good: they must express the personality both of the writer and of the recipient.
—E. M. FORSTER

• • •

I have received no more than one or two letters in my life that were worth the postage.
—HENRY DAVID THOREAU

• • •

Please write again soon. Though my own life is filled with activity, letters encourage momentary escape into others lives and I come back to my own with greater contentment.
—ELIZABETH FORSYTHE HAILEY

• • •

What a lot we lost when we stopped writing letters. You can't reread a phone call.
—LIZ CARPENTER

• • •

Sir, more than kisses, letters mingle souls; for, thus friends absent speak.
—JOHN DONNE

• • •

A letter is a blessing, a great and all-too-rare privilege that can turn a private moment into an exalted experience.
—ALEXANDRA STODDARD

• • •

We lay aside letters never to read them again, and at last we destroy them out of discretion, and so disappears the most beautiful, the most immediate breath of life, irrecoverable for ourselves and for others.
—JOHANN WOLFGANG VON GOETHE

• • •

A woman's best love letters are always written to the man she is betraying.
—LAWRENCE DURRELL

• • •

When a man sends you an impudent letter, sit right down and give it back to him with interest ten times compounded, and then throw both letters in the wastebasket.
—L. RON HUBBARD

• • •

A letter always seemed to me like immortality because it is the mind alone without corporeal friend.
—EMILY DICKINSON

• • •

If you must reread old love letters, better pick a room without mirrors.
—MIGNON MCLAUGHLIN

• • •

Samuel Johnson, *iStockphoto, Thinkstock*

The tender word forgotten,
The letter you did not write,
The flower you might have sent, dear,
Are your haunting ghosts tonight.
—MARGARET ELIZABETH SANGSTER

• • •

The age of technology has both revived the use of writing and provided ever more reasons for its spiritual solace. Emails are letters, after all, more lasting than phone calls, even if many of them r 2 cursory 4 u.
—ANNA QUINDLEN

• • •

It does me good to write a letter which is not a response to a demand, a gratuitous letter, so to speak, which has accumulated in me like the waters of a reservoir.
—HENRY MILLER

• • •

I consider it a good rule for letter-writing to leave unmentioned what the recipient already knows, and instead tell him something new.
—SIGMUND FREUD

• • •

I have made this letter longer than usual, only because I have not had the time to make it shorter.
—BLAISE PASCAL

• • •

Many people believe letters the most personal and revealing form of communication. In them, we expect to find the charmer at his nap, slumped, open-mouthed, profoundly himself without thought for appearances. Yet, this is not quite true. Letters are above all useful as a means of expressing the ideal self; and no other method of communication is quite so good for this purpose. In conversation, those uneasy eyes upon you, those lips ready with an emendation before you have begun to speak, are a powerful deterrent to unreality, even to hope. In letters we can reform without practice, beg without humiliation, snip and shape embarrassing experiences to the measure of our own desires . . .
—ELIZABETH HARDWICK

• • •

Letters are among the most significant memorial a person can leave behind them.
—JOHANN WOLFGANG VON GOETHE

• • •

chapter six

"Save the Tale": Editors and Critics

There is probably no hell for authors in the next world—they
suffer so much from critics and publishers in this.
—C. N. BOVEE

• • •

You ask for the distinction between 'Editor' and 'Publisher': an
editor selects manuscripts; a publisher selects editors.
—MAX SCHUSTER [CO-FOUNDER OF THE SIMON &
SCHUSTER PUBLISHING EMPIRE]

• • •

There is a difference between a book of two hundred pages from the very beginning, and a book of two hundred pages which is the result of an original eight hundred pages. The six hundred are there. Only you don't see them.
—ELIE WIESEL

• • •

Asking a working writer what he thinks about critics is like asking a lamppost how it feels about dogs.
—CHRISTOPHER HAMPTON

• • •

If you show someone something you've written, you give them a sharpened stake, lie down in your coffin, and say, 'When you're ready'.
—DAVID MITCHELL

• • •

Writing criticism is to writing fiction and poetry as hugging the shore is to sailing in the open sea.
—JOHN UPDIKE

• • •

A good many young writers make the mistake of enclosing a stamped, self-addressed envelope, big enough for the manuscript to come back in. This is too much of a temptation to the editor.
—RING LARDNER

• • •

The purpose of a writer is to be read, and the criticism which would destroy the power of pleasing must be blown aside.
—SAMUEL JOHNSON

• • •

There were creative writing teachers long before there were creative writing courses, and they were called and continue to be called editors.
—KURT VONNEGUT

• • •

Your manuscript is both good and original, but the part that is good is not original, and the part that is original is not good.
—SAMUEL JOHNSON

• • •

Nathaniel Hawthorne, *iStockphoto, Thinkstock*

No passion in the world is equal to the passion to alter
someone else's draft.
—H. G. WELLS

• • •

Never trust the artist. Trust the tale. The proper function of a
critic is to save the tale from the artist who created it.
—D. H. LAWRENCE

• • •

Some editors are failed writers, but so are most writers.
—T. S. ELIOT

• • •

Beware of the man who denounces woman writers; his penis
is tiny and he cannot spell.
—ERICA JONG

• • •

Try to preserve an author's style if he is an author and
has a style.
—WOLCOTT GIBBS [ON THE ROLE OF AN EDITOR]

• • •

This manuscript of yours that has just come back from another editor is a precious package. Don't consider it rejected. Consider that you've addressed it 'to the editor who can appreciate my work' and it has simply come back stamped 'Not at this address'. Just keep looking for the right address.
—BARBARA KINGSOLVER

• • •

An editor is someone who separates the wheat from the chaff and then prints the chaff.
—ADLAI STEVENSON

• • •

The reason 99% of all stories written are not bought by editors is very simple. Editors *never* buy manuscripts that are left on the closet shelf at home.
—JOHN CAMPBELL

• • •

Don't be dismayed by the opinions of editors, or critics. They are only the traffic cops of the arts.
—GENE FOWLER

• • •

Editors also know that the people who are really readers want to read. They hunger to read. They will forgive a vast number of clumsiness and scamped work of every sort if the author will delight them just enough to keep them able to continue.
—WILLIAM SLOANE

• • •

The faults of a writer of acknowledged excellence are more dangerous, because the influence of his example is more extensive; and the interest of learning requires that they should be discovered and stigmatized, before they have the sanction of antiquity conferred upon them, and become precedents of indisputable authority.
—SAMUEL JOHNSON

• • •

Rejection slips, or form letters, however tactfully phrased, are lacerations of the soul, if not quite inventions of the devil—but there is no way around them.
—ISAAC ASIMOV

• • •

Children read books, not reviews. They don't give a hoot about critics.
—ISAAC BASHEVIS SINGER

• • •

Ralph Waldo Emerson, *iStockphoto, Thinkstock*

Attacking bad books is not only a waste of time but also bad for the character. If I find a book really bad, the only interest I can derive from writing about it has to come from myself, from such display of intelligence, wit and malice as I can contrive. One cannot review a bad book without showing off.
—W. H. AUDEN

• • •

[Editors] drive us nuts. We go from near-worshipful groveling when we submit to bitter cursing when they reject us.
—KEN RAND

• • •

An editor should tell the author his writing is better than it is. Not a lot better, a little better.
—T. S. ELIOT

• • •

Would you convey my compliments to the purist who reads your proofs and tell him or her that I write in a sort of broken-down patois which is something like the way a Swiss waiter talks, and that when I split an infinitive, God damn it, I split it so it will stay split, and when I interrupt the velvety smoothness of my more or less literate syntax with a few sudden words of bar-room vernacular, that is done with the eyes wide open and the mind relaxed but attentive.
—RAYMOND CHANDLER

• • •

Editing is the same as quarreling with writers—same thing exactly.
—HAROLD ROSS

• • •

What a blessed thing it is that nature, when she invented, manufactured and patented her authors, contrived to make critics out of the chips that were left!
—OLIVER WENDELL HOLMES

• • •

The road to ignorance is paved with good editors.
—GEORGE BERNARD SHAW

• • •

Honest criticism is hard to take, particularly from a relative, a friend, an acquaintance, or a stranger.
—FRANKLIN JONES

• • •

If critics say your work stinks it's because they want it to stink and they can make it stink by scaring you into conformity with their comfortable little standards. Standards so low that they can no longer be considered "dangerous" but set in place in their compartmental understandings.
—JACK KEROUAC

• • •

Critics ought never to be consulted, but while errors may yet be rectified or insipidity suppressed. But when the book has once been dismissed into the world, and can be no more retouched, I know not whether a very different conduct should not be prescribed, and whether firmness and spirit may not sometimes be of use to overpower arrogance and repel brutality.

—SAMUEL JOHNSON

• • •

When you send off a short story, it sits on the editor's desk in the same pile with stories by the most famous and honored names in present-day writing—and it's not going to be accepted unless it's as good as theirs. (And it'll probably have to be better.)

—DANIEL QUINN

• • •

Editor: A person employed by a newspaper, whose business it is to separate the wheat from the chaff, and to see that the chaff is printed.

—L. RON HUBBARD

• • •

A critic is a man who knows the way but can't drive the car.

—KENNETH TYNAN

• • •

Walt Whitman, *iStockphoto, Thinkstock*

From the moment I picked your book up until I laid it down I
was convulsed with laughter. Some day I intend reading it.
—GROUCHO MARX

• • •

A critic knows more than the author he criticizes, or just as
much, or at least somewhat less.
—CARDINAL HENRY MANNING

• • •

A certain critic—for such men, I regret to say, do exist—made
the nasty remark about my last novel that it contained 'all
the old Wodehouse characters under different names.' He
has probably by now been eaten by bears, like the children
who made mock of the prophet Elisha: but if he still survives
he will not be able to make a similar charge against Summer
Lightning. With my superior intelligence, I have out-gener-
alled the man this time by putting in all the old Wodehouse
characters under the same names. Pretty silly it will make him
feel, I rather fancy.
—P. G. WODEHOUSE

• • •

Pay no attention to what the critics say; no statue has ever
been erected to a critic.
—JEAN SIBELIUS

• • •

The diversion of baiting an author has the sanction of all ages and nations, and is more lawful than the sport of teasing other animals, because, for the most part, he comes voluntarily to the stake, furnished, as he imagines, by the patron powers of literature, with resistless weapons, and impenetrable armour, with the mail of the boar of Erymanth, and the paws of the lion of Nemea.
—SAMUEL JOHNSON

• • •

Editing should be, especially in the case of old writers, a counseling rather than a collaborating task. The tendency of the writer-editor to collaborate is natural, but he should say to himself, How can I help this writer to say it better in his own style? and avoid How can I show him how I would write it, if it were my piece?
—JAMES THURBER

• • •

With all editing, no matter how sensitive—and I've been very lucky here—I react sulkily at first, but then I settle down and get on with it, and a year later I have my book in my hand.
—MICHAEL MORPURGO

• • •

"And I'll tell you," he interrupted. "The chief qualification of ninety-nine per cent of all editors is failure. They have failed as writers. Don't think they prefer the drudgery of the desk and the slavery to their circulation and to the business manager to the joy of writing. They have tried to write, and they have failed. And right there is the cursed paradox of it. Every portal to success in literature is guarded by those watch-dogs, the failures in literature. The editors, sub-editors, associate editors, most of them, and the manuscript-readers for the magazines and book publishers, most of them, nearly all of them, are men who wanted to write and who have failed. And yet they, of all creatures under the sun the most unfit, are the very creatures who decide what shall and what shall not find its way into print—they, who have proved themselves not original, who have demonstrated that they lack the divine fire, sit in judgment upon originality and genius. And after them come the reviewers, just so many more failures. Don't tell me that they have not dreamed the dream and attempted to write poetry or fiction; for they have, and they have failed. Why, the average review is more nauseating than cod-liver oil. But you know my opinion on the reviewers and the alleged critics. There are great critics, but they are as rare as comets. If I fail as a writer, I shall have proved for the career of editorship. There's bread and butter and jam, at any rate."

—JACK LONDON [FROM *MARTIN EDEN*]

• • •

Never throw up on an editor.
—ELLEN DATLOW

• • •

Oliver Wendell Holmes, Sr., *iStockphoto, Thinkstock*

chapter seven

"No Man but a Blockhead": Writing for Money

Writing is like prostitution. First you do it for love, and then
for a few close friends, and then for money.
—MOLIÈRE

• • •

No man but a blockhead ever wrote, except for money.
—SAMUEL JOHNSON

• • •

Instead of marveling with Johnson, how anything but profit should incite men to literary labor, I am rather surprised that mere emolument should induce them to labor so well.
—THOMAS GREEN [IN RESPONSE TO JOHNSON]

• • •

Write without pay until somebody offers to pay.
—MARK TWAIN

• • •

I think of an author as somebody who goes into the marketplace and puts down his rug and says, "I will tell you a story," and then he passes the hat.
—ROBERTSON DAVIES

• • •

If you want to get rich from writing, write the sort of thing that's read by persons who move their lips when they're reading to themselves.
—DON MARQUIS

• • •

The first chapter sells the book; the last chapter sells the next book.
—MICKEY SPILLANE

• • •

The only reason for being a professional writer is that you just
can't help it.
—LEO ROSTEN

• • •

Writing is a crummy profession, but a good hobby.
—PAAVO HAAVIKKO

• • •

I've always believed in writing without a collaborator, because
when two people are writing the same book, each believes he
gets all the worries and only half the royalties.
—AGATHA CHRISTIE

• • •

Writing is turning one's worst moments into money.
—J. P. DONLEAVY

• • •

Why do I write? Well, let's see… that's a tough one. Oh, okay, I
know. Money. If I were not getting paid, I would never write—
except perhaps when answering personal ads from hot, lonely
co-eds. Aside from the money, there are very few advantages
to being a writer. Only the stupidest of actresses sleeps with
the writer.
—LEE ARONSOHN

• • •

Most writers can write books faster than publishers can write checks.
—RICHARD CURTIS

• • •

We write to taste life twice, in the moment and in retrospection.
—ANAIS NIN

• • •

I never write 'metropolis' for seven cents when I can write 'city' and get paid the same.
—MARK TWAIN

• • •

Stories may well be lies, but they are good lies that say true things, and which can sometimes pay the rent.
—NEIL GAIMAN

• • •

If you're a freelance writer and aren't used to being ignored, neglected, and generally given short shrift, you must not have been in the business very long.
—POPPY Z. BRITE

• • •

There's no money in poetry, but then there's no poetry in money either.
—ROBERT GRAVES

• • •

Writing for a penny a word is ridiculous. If a man wanted to make a million dollars, the best way would be to start his own religion.
—L. RON HUBBARD

• • •

If you try to please audiences, uncritically accepting their tastes, it can only mean that you have no respect for them: that you simply want to collect their money.
—ANDREI TARKOVSKY

• • •

One fact us inescapable: until the screenwriter does his job, nobody else can do theirs. Until the screenwriter does his job, nobody else has a job.
—ROBERT TOWNE

• • •

Alphonse de Lamartine *Zoonar, Thinkstock*

Writing is the hardest way of earning a living, with the possible exception of wrestling alligators.
—OLIN MILLER

• • •

Almost anyone can be an author; the business is to collect money and fame from this state of being.
—A. A. MILNE

• • •

In the same way that a woman becomes a prostitute. First I did it to please myself, then I did it to please my friends, and finally I did it for money.
—MOLIÈRE [ASKED ABOUT HOW HE BECAME A WRITER]

• • •

Writing is the only profession where no one considers you ridiculous if you earn no money.
—JULES RENARD

• • •

Writing isn't generally a lucrative source of income; only a few, exceptional writers reach the income levels associated with the best-sellers. Rather, most of us write because we can make a modest living, or even supplement our day jobs, doing something about which we feel passionately. Even at the worst of times, when nothing goes right, when the prose is clumsy and the ideas feel stale, at least we're doing something that we genuinely love. There's no other reason to work this hard, except that love.
—MELISSA SCOTT

• • •

Writers should never try to outguess the marketplace in search of a salable idea; the simple truth is that all good books will eventually find a publisher if the writer tries hard enough, and a central secret to writing a good book is to write one that people like you will enjoy.
—RICHARD NORTH PATTERSON

• • •

The only two kinds of books could earn an American writer a living are cookbooks and detective novels.
—REX STOUT

• • •

The only reason for being a professional writer is that you can't help it.
—LEO ROSTEN

• • •

What is a screenplay? 120 pages of begging for money
and attention.
—JAMES SCHAMUS

• • •

I got to thinking about the point in every freelancer's life
where he has to decide whether he wants to A, have a social
life, and do art in his spare time, or B, do art, and have a social
life in his spare time. It has always seemed to me that if you
have any hope of making a living as an artist—writer, musician, whatever—you absolutely must learn to tell people to
leave you alone, and to mean it, and to eject them from your
life if they don't respect that. This is necessary not because
your job is more important than anyone else's—it isn't—but
because a great many people will think of you as not having a
job. 'Oh, how wonderful—you can work whenever you want
to!' Well, yes, to a point, but generally 'whenever you want to'
had better be most of the time, or else you won't have a roof
over your head.
—POPPY Z. BRITE

• • •

I never had any doubts about my abilities. I knew I could
write. I just had to figure out how to eat while doing this.
—CORMAC MCCARTHY

• • •

Johann Wolfgang von Goethe, *Zoonar, Thinkstock*

chapter eight

"Open a Vein": A Smile or Two Along with Some Good Advice

I try to leave out the parts that people skip.
—ELMORE LEONARD

• • •

There's nothing to writing. All you do is sit down at a typewriter and open a vein.
—RED SMITH

• • •

Writing is easy; all you do is sit staring at a blank sheet of paper until the drops of blood form on your forehead.
—GENE FOWLER

• • •

Do not place a photograph of your favourite author on your desk, especially if the author is one of the famous ones who committed suicide.
—RODDY DOYLE

• • •

Marry somebody you love and who thinks you being a writer's a good idea.
—RICHARD FORD

• • •

I love being a writer. What I can't stand is the paperwork.
—PETER DE VRIES

• • •

Poets aren't very useful. Because they aren't consumeful or very produceful.
—OGDEN NASH

• • •

I take the view, and always have, that if you cannot say what you are going to say in twenty minutes you ought to go away and write a book about it.
—LORD BRABAZON

• • •

When I finish a first draft, it's always just as much of a mess as it's always been. I still make the same mistakes every time.
—MICHAEL CHABON

• • •

Most writers regard truth as their most valuable possession, and therefore are most economical in its use.
—MARK TWAIN

• • •

"What are American dry-goods?" asked the duchess, raising her large hands in wonder and accentuating the verb. "American novels," answered Lord Henry.
—OSCAR WILDE

• • •

Writing is a fairly lonely business unless you invite people in to watch you do it, which is often distracting and then have to ask them to leave.
—MARC LAWRENCE

• • •

Fyodor Dostoyevsky, *iStockphoto, Thinkstock*

There are two kinds of writer: those that make you think, and those that make you wonder.
—BRIAN ALDISS

• • •

If you figure out how to make pictures without writers, let me know.
—IRVING THALBERG

• • •

English usage is sometimes more than mere taste, judgment and education—sometimes it's sheer luck, like getting across the street.
—E. B. WHITE

• • •

Originality does not consist in saying what no one has ever said before, but in saying exactly what you think yourself.
—JAMES F. STEPHAN

• • •

I write to discover what I think. After all, the bars aren't open that early.
—DANIEL J. BOORSTIN

• • •

The art of writing is the art of applying the seat of the pants to the seat of the chair.
—MARY HEATON VORSE

• • •

Idling reader, you may believe me when I tell you that I should have liked this book, which is the child of my brain, to be the fairest, the sprightliest and the cleverest that could be imagined, but I have not been able to contravene the law of nature which would have it that like begets like.
—MIGUEL DE CERVANTES

• • •

The wastepaper basket is the writer's best friend.
—ISAAC BASHEVIS SINGER

• • •

It took me fifteen years to discover I had no talent for writing, but I couldn't give it up because by that time I was too famous.
—ROBERT BENCHLEY

• • •

The most essential gift for a good writer is a built-in, shock-proof, shit detector. This is the writer's radar and all great writers have had it.
—ERNEST HEMINGWAY

• • •

If the sex scene doesn't make you want to do it—whatever it is they're doing—it hasn't been written right.
—SLOAN WILSON

• • •

It's hell writing and it's hell not writing. The only tolerable state is having just written.
—ROBERT HASS

• • •

People are certainly impressed by the aura of creative power which a writer may wear, but can easily demolish it with a few well-chosen questions. Bob Shaw has observed that the deadliest questions usually come as a pair: "Have you published anything?"—loosely translated as: I've never heard of you—and "What name do you write under?"—loosely translatable as: I've definitely never heard of you.
—BRIAN STABLEFORD

• • •

My books are water; those of the great geniuses are wine. Everybody drinks water.
—MARK TWAIN

• • •

Henry David Thoreau, *iStockphoto, Thinkstock*

All of us learn to write in the second grade. Most of us go on
to greater things.
—BOBBY KNIGHT

• • •

If you would shut your door against the children for an hour
a day and say: 'Mother is working on her five-act tragedy in
blank verse!' you would be surprised how they would respect
you. They would probably all become playwrights.
—BRENDA UELAND

• • •

One should not be too severe on English novels; they are the
only relaxation of the intellectually unemployed.
—OSCAR WILDE

• • •

Beware of writers who tell you how hard they work. (Beware
of anybody who tries to tell you that.) Writing is indeed often
dark and lonely, but no one really has to do it. Yes, writing
can be complicated, exhausting, isolating, abstracting, boring,
dulling, briefly exhilarating; it can be made to be grueling and
demoralizing. And occasionally it can produce rewards. But
it's never as hard as, say, piloting an L-1011 into O'Hare on a
snowy night in January, or doing brain surgery when you have

to stand up for 10 hours straight, and once you start you can't just stop. If you're a writer, you can stop anywhere, any time, and no one will care or ever know. Plus, the results might be better if you do.
—RICHARD FORD

• • •

Write quickly and you will never write well; write well, and you will soon write quickly.
—MARCUS FABIUS QUINTILIANUS

• • •

Every journalist has a novel in him, which is an excellent place for it.
—RUSSELL LYNES

• • •

Finishing a book is just like you took a child out in the back yard and shot it.
—TRUMAN CAPOTE

• • •

There comes a moment in the day, when you have written your pages in the morning, attended to your correspondence in the afternoon, and have nothing further to do. Then comes the hour when you are bored; that's the time for sex.
—H. G. WELLS

• • •

I'm writing a book. I've got the page numbers done.
—STEPHEN WRIGHT

• • •

Life is what happens to a writer between drafts.
—DAMON MILLER

• • •

Mr. Henry James writes fiction as if it were a painful duty.
—OSCAR WILDE

• • •

A young musician plays scales in his room and only bores his family. A beginning writer, on the other hand, sometimes has the misfortune of getting into print.
—MARGUERITE YOURCENAR

• • •

I love deadlines. I like the whooshing sound they make as they fly by.
—DOUGLAS ADAMS

• • •

Your life story would not make a good book. Don't even try.
—FRAN LEBOWITZ

• • •

Sophocles, *iStockphoto, Thinkstock*

I write to discover what I think. After all, the bars aren't open that early.
—DANIEL J. BOORSTIN [EXPLAINING WHY HE WROTE EARLY IN THE MORNING]

• • •

Read your compositions, and whenever you come across a passage which you think is particularly fine, strike it out.
—SAMUEL JOHNSON

• • •

If a book is not alive in the writer's mind, it is as dead as year-old horse-shit.
—STEPHEN KING

• • •

When you take stuff from one writer, it's plagiarism; but when you take it from many writers, it's research.
—WILLIAM MIZNER

• • •

The problem with patches of purple prose is not that they are purple, but they are patches.
—VIRGINIA WOOLF

• • •

Sometimes she thought he was a big fountain pen which was always sucking at her blood for ink.
—D. H. LAWRENCE, [FROM "NEW EVE AND OLD ADAM"]

• • •

Writing is the best way to talk without being interrupted.
—JULES RENARD

• • •

I used to have a pet theory that a lot of writers were good at something else, often a sport or another activity, and then fell short of quite being good enough. And that was certainly the case with me and tap-dancing.
—ZADIE SMITH

• • •

One nice thing about putting the thing away for a couple of months before looking at it is that start to appreciate your own wit. Of course, this can be carried too far. But it's kind of cool when you crack up a piece of writing, and then realize you wrote it. I recommend this feeling.
—STEVEN BRUST

• • •

I can write better than anybody who can write faster, and I can write faster than anybody who can write better.
—A. J. LIEBLING

• • •

A person who publishes a book appears willfully in public eye with his pants down.
—EDNA ST. VINCENT MILLAY

• • •

A blank piece of paper is God's way of telling us how hard it is to be God.
—SIDNEY SHELDON

• • •

Writing is the flip side of sex—it's good only when it's over.
—HUNTER S. THOMPSON

• • •

Or don't you like to write letters. I do because it's such a swell way to keep from working and yet feel you've done something.
—ERNEST HEMINGWAY

• • •

Dante Alighieri, *iStockphoto, Thinkstock*

There's no such thing as writer's block. That was invented by people in California who couldn't write.
—TERRY PRATCHETT

• • •

I get up in the morning, torture a typewriter until it screams, then stop.
—CLARENCE BUDINGTON KELLAND

• • •

When my horse is running good, I don't stop to give him sugar.
—WILLIAM FAULKNER

• • •

Having been unpopular in high school is not just cause for book publication.
—FRAN LEBOWITZ

• • •

Either a writer doesn't want to talk about his work, or he talks about it more than you want.
—ANATOLE BROYARD

• • •

Sometimes you have to go on when you don't feel like it, and sometimes you're doing good work when it feels like all you're managing is to shovel shit from a sitting position.
—STEPHEN KING

• • •

It is perfectly okay to write garbage—as long as you edit brilliantly.
—C. J. CHERRYH

• • •

Television has raised writing to a new low.
—SAMUEL GOLDWYN

• • •

I just sit at a typewriter and curse a bit.
—P. G. WODEHOUSE [WHEN ASKED ABOUT HIS WRITING TECHNIQUE]

• • •

The profession of book-writing makes horse racing seem like a solid, stable business.
—JOHN STEINBECK

• • •

Robert Burns, *iStockphoto, Thinkstock*

Only a mediocre writer is always at his best.
—W. SOMERSET MAUGHAM

• • •

All the words I use in my stories can be found in the dictionary—it's just a matter of arranging them into the right sentences.
—W. SOMERSET MAUGHAM

• • •

A writer will seal his own coffin,
And the interests of readers will soften,
If the author insists
On the usual twists,
And he goes to the Wells once too often.
—MARK GRENIER

• • •